Contents

Developing with Google App Engine

by Eugene Ciurana

Large scale, high availability application development was a dark art until the release of Google App Engine. It involved balancing (and sometimes pitting) the programmers' skills against the application requirements and the underlying infrastructure. Google App Engine frees us, the developers, from most concerns about the infrastructure so that we can focus on coding and delivering useful software. It empowers us to develop complex applications with a simple and elegant API, using robust programming tools like Python, and leveraging the sophisticated data storage, searching and caching technologies that helped Google to succeed. This is cloud computing made easy and it enables us to create high availability Software as a Service without excessive overhead or infrastructure worries. This book is about how to design, build, deploy, and manage Google App Engine applications efficiently.

This work would not have been possible without the support from Apress, the Google App Engine team, and the members of various IRC groups. My special thanks go to Richard Ables, Richard L. Burton III, Guillermo Castro, Charles Kolya Colt, Johan Edstrom, Jason Essington, Aaron Gallagher, Bennett Hiles, Nick Heudecker, Devin Jeanpierre, Shane Jonson, Heather Lang, Justin Lee, Joe Littlefeatherstein, Andrew Lombardi, Marzia Niccolai, Joseph Ottinger, Jeffrey Pepper, Pranav Prakash, Sverre Rabbelier, Tracy Snell, Craig Tataryn, Nestor Toro, Jason Whaley, and Grace Wong.

Thanks to the denizens of the #appengine and #python IRC channels from Freenode.net, who always replied to my endless Python-specific questions without losing their patience.

Developing with Google App Engine *está dedicado a Cary Macías con mucho cariño. ¡Gracias Jefa!*

Chapter 1: Google App Engine

This chapter provides an introduction to Google App Engine concepts. We'll look at development methodology and how App Engine implements cloud computing concepts by providing both development and runtime services.

What Is Google App Engine?

Google App Engine is a Python-based runtime platform that provides web application hosting, data storage, and high-speed networking by running on top of Google's massive infrastructure.

Developers can use the preview release of the Google App Engine API and serve applications free of charge or obligation, with some restrictions:

- They're limited to 5 million page views per month (bandwith and CPU usage).

- They can consume only 500 MB of persistent storage.

Note   At the time of this writing, Google App Engine is available only as a free preview, and no pricing plans have been announced yet.

The restrictions aren't bad considering the upside:

- Development takes place in the end users' local environment, and OS X, Linux, and Windows are all supported.

- Google App Engine provides efficient dynamic web application execution, even under load or with heavy data usage, thanks to built-in scaling and load balancing.

- The persistent storage system supports transactions, queries, and sorting.

- E-mail support uses the Gmail API for authentication and e-mail support.

The runtime is abstracted away from the underlying operating system to avoid platform dependencies. The Google infrastructure provides automatic, on-demand traffic shaping and load balancing for your application by distributing it across multiple servers. Each application also runs in its own secure sandbox, independent of other applications and potential resource conflicts. Applications can be hosted in a default `appspot.com` domain or in your own Google Apps account. Getting applications up and running involves only minor setup work.

Google App Engine and Cloud Computing

Cloud or utility computing describes applications running on distributed, computing resources owned and operated by a third party. Some cloud computing providers offer general-purpose computing and storage capabilities, while others provide dedicated or specialized services.

End User Applications on the Cloud

End user applications are the most noticeable cloud computing examples. They utilize the Software as a Service (SaaS) and Platform as a Service (PaaS) computing models. Users interact with applications over standard web browsers without concern about deployment or in-house administration.

Services on the Cloud

Rather than delivering interactive applications, providers deliver APIs in the form of services or service-enabling platforms over standard communications or data exchange protocols. These services may also include hosting systems as part of their offerings. Some cloud services include:

- *Web services*: Salesforce.com, the United States Postal Service, and Google Maps all offer discrete APIs for accomplishing specific tasks.

- *Service platforms*: Mule, Postini, SecureWorks, and Cape Clear provide integration capabilities for bridging enterprise systems with third-party service providers or end user applications over ESB technology.

- *Managed services*: Sun Microsystems, IBM, Liquid Computing, and 3Tera offer hosted services that include a combination of end user and services software along with the hardware infrastructure and even IT teams for support.

Google App Engine and the Cloud

App Engine offers three distinct sets of cloud computing features to the end user:

- A PaaS that development teams and organizations may use for building public or in-house web applications that support transactions, uniform authentication, and robust scalability and availability

- Applications created with Google App Engine that are offered as SaaS, consumed directly from the end-users' web browsers

- The ability to integrate or consume third-party web services from other service platforms

So how do you start implementing cloud computing applications? The rest of this chapter describes how Google App Engine makes the task quite simple.

Before You Start Using App Engine

You should know a few basic things before getting started with Google App Engine:

- Some Python programming (the more the better!)

- Basic understanding of how web applications are built and how they behave at runtime, including use of CGI, servlets, and application containers

- How to query and update a database using SQL commands

Ease of use is one of App Engine's main design goals. Code can be unit tested and exercised within an App Engine emulator that comes with the software development kit (SDK) or in stand-alone Python code snippets. The interpreted nature of Python allows for quick command line testing and prototyping. The hardware requirements for the SDK and App Engine emulator are minimal, so even someone with a modest workstation and a basic Internet connection can get to work right away.

Tip   *Dive into Python* by Mark Pilgrim (Apress, 2004) is a great way to learn this programming language, from basic to advanced concepts. The book is available in print and online at `http://www.diveintopython.org`.

App Engine applications with user interactivity require support of a web application framework. The Python Web Server Gateway Interface (WSGI) is a standard mechanism that web servers and application servers will use for communicating with your application. App Engine supports WSGI and will work with any compatible application server. You may want to read about WSGI for background, though application server integration will be covered in Chapter 4.

Setting Up Your Development Environment

The development and deployment environment is a combination of App Engine services on the web and a SDK that you will download to your workstation. Google requires an account that will tie your environment to other services like Google Docs or Gmail. You can register and get the SDK at `http://code.google.com/appengine`. Follow these steps to get started:

1. Ensure that your development workstation has Python 2.5 (or later) installed. Open a console and enter the command `python --version`.

2. Define an application to begin.

3. Provide a mobile number to which Google will send an SMS confirmation message; you will need the confirmation code in order to proceed.

4. Create an application identifier and an application used for constructing a URL in the form `yourappid.appspot.com`. The examples for this book will use `genpasswd` and `bookmarksbin` as the application ID. You can set other options, such as end-user access and authentication (see Chapter 8).

5. Install the SDK appropriate for your development platform. Downloads for OS X, Linux, and Windows are available from `http://code.google.com/appengine/downloads.html`.

6. Start `GoogleAppEngineLauncher` to finish the installation. The launcher for OS X and Windows requires your administrator password, because it sets symlinks to the local application server emulator and the upload tools (`/usr/local/bin` for OS X) and creates a home directory (`/usr/local/google_appengine`) for the SDK itself. This is a one-time installation, and the launcher won't need the administration password again.

7. Ensure that the local application server emulator and upload tools are globally executable by running the following commands:

   - `dev_appserver.py -help`

   - `appcfg.py -help`

8. Check that both Python and App Engine tool installation directories are in your `PATH` environment variable: `which dev_appserver.py` on OS X and Linux, for example. You should see something like `/usr/local/bin/dev_appserver.py`, and `set | grep PATH` should show `/usr/local/bin`.

You are ready to start coding and managing App Engine projects!

Hello, World!

App Engine applications are structured in your file system in the same way that they'll be set up in the Google servers after you upload them. A project requires at least one Python program and a YAML file that tells the hosting web server how to run and present your application in response to user requests.

> ## WHAT IS YAML?
>
> YAML is a cross-language, human-friendly, data-serialization language used for configuration files, persistence, and network messaging. YAML is easier to read by humans and consumes fewer runtime resources than XML. "YAML" stands for "YAML Ain't a Markup Language," and you can find out more about it at `http://yaml.org`.

Create a directory called `greetingprogram`, and in it, save the `greeting.py` file shown in Listing 1-1.

Listing 1-1. greeting.py

```
# Greeting program
print 'Content-Type: text/plain'
print ''
print 'Hello, World!'
```

The only bit worth noting about this program is that it needs to tell the web server what kind of content it will deliver. You'll see how to deal with that by using a WSGI framework in Chapters 2 and 3 so that we don't have to do that every time that you code something.

Listing 1-2 shows the runtime metadata defined in YAML for your new application. The `app.yaml` name is used by convention, because the web server seeks it when starting your application. Using a different file name results in an `AppConfigNotFoundError`.

Listing 1-2. app.yaml

```
application: greetingprogram
version: 1
runtime: python
api_version: 1

handlers:
 - url: /.*
   script: greeting.py
```

Open your system shell, go to your development directory, and enter the following command:

```
dev_appserver.py greetingprogram/
```

That starts the application server and shows the server's log in your console. `greetingprogram/` is the directory that contains your Python and YAML files. You should see this message if all is well:

```
Running application greetingprogram on port 8080:
 http://localhost:8080
```

Finally, point your web browser at this address, and validate your greeting program, as shown in Figure 1-1.

Figure 1-1. Output from greeting.py

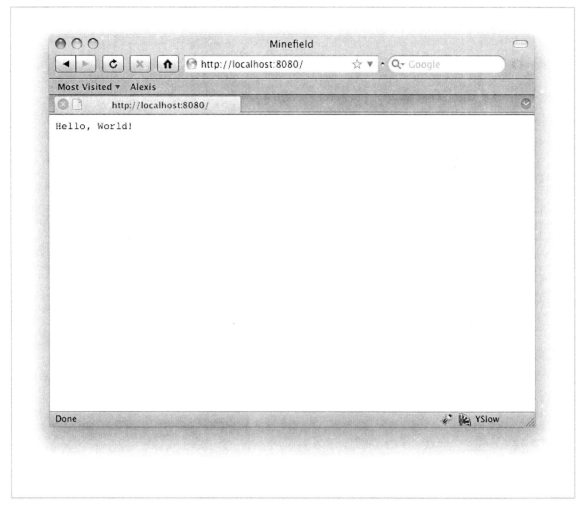

Summary

The Google App Engine is a Platform as a Service (PaaS) application framework for developing end-user Software as a Service (SaaS) that runs on Google's massive servers and leverages their scalable infrastructure. App Engine is designed so that even developers with minimal Python and web development experience can quickly write and deploy sophisticated applications. App Engine simplifies cloud application development and complements other cloud computing platforms with an end-user application model that's easy to roll out.

The greeting program was a trivial application. How do you go about authoring a complete project and publishing it to the Web? You'll gain experience in using the development tools by exploring the SDK in Chapter 2.

Chapter 2: Exploring the SDK

An App Engine project consists of several files that handle all aspects of the application. This chapter presents a strong password generation application to introduce the project layout, configuration requirements, the local development web server, debugging techniques, and techniques for publishing the application to the web.

Creating Your First Complete Project

A complete application consists of most or all of these files:

- The Python scripts that implement the program logic

- The app.yaml file that describes the application's runtime configuration parameters

- Any static content such as graphics, HTML, and CSS

UPDATING THE SDK

Google updates the SDK often to patch bugs or to add new functionality. The upgrade methodology varies from one system to the next, but overall, it's quite simple and straightforward to upgrade:

- Download the upgrade.

- Mount the disk image (Mac) or decompress the package (Linux or Windows), and copy or extract the App Engine launcher to your development environment. The launcher won't work from the mounted disk image or from a zipped directory.

- Run the launcher until the process completes.

Updates are backward compatible and nondestructive. Any applications already on the disk will be unaffected.

Development will take place in the development web server that ships with the SDK. The local server is smart enough to detect changes to any of the files being worked on, and it reloads them before serving any requests involving them.

The application launcher can create a basic set of project files to simplify development. Figure 2-1 shows the creation of the GenPasswd application in this user's App Engine development directory, which the user created.

Figure 2-1. New project created via the App Engine Launcher

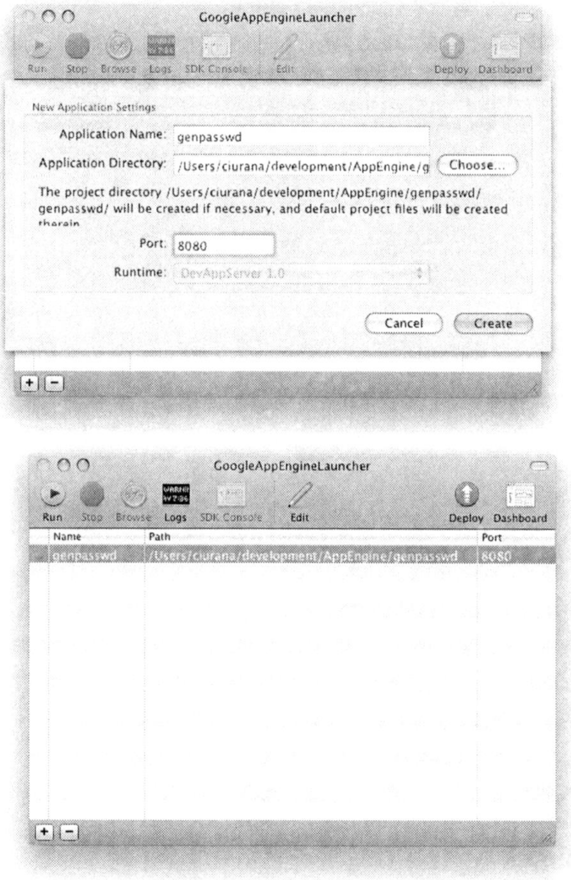

Caution The launcher automatically generates any project name that you want, but it doesn't validate it against the App Engine's requirements. Ensure that project names are made of all lowercase letters, dashes, and digits. The App Engine validates them using this regular expression: '^(?!-)[a-z\d\-]{1,100}$'. Invalid names will result in a configuration error when trying to load the application.

Listing 2-1 shows that the launcher doesn't produce scaffolding; it only provides the bare bones files for an application.

Listing 2-1. Automatically Generated main.py for GenPasswd

```
import wsgiref.handlers

from google.appengine.ext import webapp

class MainHandler(webapp.RequestHandler):

  def get(self):
  self.response.out.write('Hello world!')


def main():
  application = webapp.WSGIApplication(
            [('/', MainHandler)],
            debug=True
          )

  wsgi.handlers.CGIHandler().run(application)


if __name__ == '__main__':
  main()
```

The program won't run in a regular Python interpreter because it requires the App Engine's libraries. Start the development server, and test your program by using your web browser or cURL to fetch `http://localhost` `:8080`. The server will reply with

```
curl -i http://localhost:8080
HTTP/1.0 200 OK
Server: Development/1.0 Python/2.5.1
Date: Tue, 05 Aug 2008 16:03:22 GMT
Content-Type: text/html; charset=utf-8
Cache-Control: no-cache
content-length: 12

Hello world!
```

Tip   The development server and the App Engine host consider the application's home directory to be the URL root location. If you receive a 404 error while trying to run this example, you may have used `http://localhost:8080/appname`, instead of `http://localhost` `:8080`.

The webapp Framework

Chapter 1 discussed the need for a web application framework for the App Engine; otherwise, the user would have to handle all the gritty details of parsing HTTP methods and manually set headers and other responses. App Engine works with any WSGI-compatible framework. For convenience, the App Engine SDK includes webapp in its standard distribution and may be used for handling web requests for an application, as seen at the top of Listing 2-1.

webapp doesn't provide a feature set like Django or other Python frameworks. It's adequate for writing nontrivial web applications, though, and is capable of handling all HTTP 1.1 requests, setting headers, managing cookies, and so on. webapp includes these objects:

- `Request`: A subclass of the WebOb `Request` class (see `http://pythonpaste.org/webob/reference.html`) that contains information about an incoming request

- `Response`: Used for sending data, status, and header information back to the caller

- `RequestHandler`: A base class that the application developer extends for processing application requests based on `Request` objects passed from a regular HTTP request

- `WSGIApplication`: The main entry point into an App Engine application that sets the request handlers and overall environment

webapp also includes a couple of useful functions in its `google.appengine.webapp.util` package:

- `run_wsgi_app (anApplication)` is similar to the wsgiref WSGI-to-CGI adapter from the standard Python library. This function is aware of the App Engine environment (it knows if the application runs in the development environment or in the Google infrastructure) and provides debugging messages to the console for message handling and application errors in ways that the standard Python CGI handler doesn't.

- `@login_required` is an annotation for verifying if the end user is logged on with a Google account. If not, it optionally redirects the user to the sign-in page.

The `util` package will see more functions added as the App Engine matures. Review the App Engine documentation often.

Using the Sandboxed Python Runtime

The selection of Python as the App Engine's preferred programming language has received an overall good welcome from the development community. Python is robust, mature, and feature rich. Using it in App Engine development requires awareness of some of the limitations implemented for the platform.

Scalability was one of Google's main design goals. Google achieved scalability through virtualization so that any one system in the Google infrastructure can run an application's code—even two consecutive requests posted to the same application may not go to the same server. Some Python features were curtailed to achieve scalability through virtualization in a sandbox specific to the App Engine infrastructure, for example:

- Some standard libraries have been disabled.

- There is no multithreading.

- Communications are limited to HTTP and HTTPS.

- Using Django and other WSGI-compatible frameworks foregoes framework features.

On the upside, any Python-only code library can be integrated with and used by an App Engine application, as long as it doesn't break the sandbox rules.

What sorts of limitations are placed on sandboxed applications? Here are some examples of things your application *can't* do:

- Make any type of system calls.

- Open a socket or other communication channel to access another system over the network. Communications are limited to URL fetches over HTTP or HTTPS.

- Write to the file system or change permissions.

- Launch new threads or subprocesses. Requests are handled in a single thread of execution within a few seconds; the App Engine may kill a process if it takes too long to respond, and "too long" isn't well defined.

However, that leaves quite a lot of things available that your sandboxed application *can* do:

- Use any pure Python third-party libraries and packages.

- Define Python packages in the application subdirectories.

- Read the file system, including any of the files uploaded with the application except for static files, which aren't kept on the file system.

- Use the App Engine datastore for persisting data.

- Make any calls to the Python standard library except for those that attempt unsafe system-level operations.

> ### WHICH NATIVE C PYTHON MODULES ARE ENABLED?
>
> View the complete list of C modules allowed by Google App Engine, including the fully supported, partially enabled, and empty ones at http://code.google.com/appengine/kb/libraries.html.

Use of a sandboxed feature may result in either successful imports, calls to empty code, or runtime exceptions, depending on the module being called.

Putting the Application Together

The main.py file was renamed to passwordgenerator.py, in accordance with the Python naming conventions. The app.yaml file also reflects this change in the URL mapping line (see Listing 2-2).

Listing 2-2. Changes to app.yaml

```
.

.
handlers:
- url: /.*
  script: passwordgenerator.py
```

The url: tag refers to valid regular expressions that can be mapped to standard URL encoded strings. The main program logic is implemented by adding event handlers as shown in Listing 2-3.

Listing 2-3. passwordgenerator.py

```python
#!/usr/bin/env python

import cgi;
import wsgiref.handlers

from google.appengine.ext import webapp
from google.appengine.ext.webapp.util \
    import run_wsgi_app

# *** Symbolic Constants ***

BASE = ord('0')

def mainForm():
  return """
    <html>
      <head>
        <title>
          GenPasswd Strong(ish) Password Generator
        </title>
      </head>
      <body>
        <div align="center">
          <h1>Strong(ish) Password Generator</h1>
          <form
            method="POST"
            name="baseWordCapture"
            action="/">
              <p>Base word (6 chars minimum):</p>
              <input type="text" name="baseWord"
                cols="24" /> <br />
              <input type="submit" />
              <input type="reset" />
```

```python
                    <p>Password:</p>
                    <p>n/a</p>
                </form>
            </div>
        </body>
    </html>
    """

class PasswordGenerator(webapp.RequestHandler):

    def __process(self, aWord):
        password = ""
        if (len(aWord) >= 6):
            for i in range(len(aWord)):
                if i in [1, 5, 8, 13, 21]:
                    password += chr(BASE+(ord(aWord[i])+i)%10)
                else:
                    password += aWord[i]

        return password

    def get(self):
        self.response.out.write(mainForm())

    def post(self):
        output    = self.response.out
        baseWord = cgi.escape(
            self.request.get('baseWord'))
        password = self.__process(baseWord)

        output.write(mainForm().replace(
            "n/a", password))

def main():
application = webapp.WSGIApplication(
        [ ('/', PasswordGenerator) ], debug=True)
```

```
    run_wsgi_app(application)


if __name__ == '__main__':
    main()
```

The program will handle CGI requests in the form of GET and POST calls. Importing the cgi module simplifies getting individual values from forms or, as in this case, escape input values and provides a safe transformation to working strings for use in the rest of the application as shown in the method POST handler.

Using Templates vs. Inline HTML

The basic HTML is built inline in the mainForm() function. The request handlers call mainForm() so the user can interact with the application. Chapter 4 discusses how to use WSGI-compatible templating engines in applications. The form handling and user output are quite simple, so using the mainForm() and a simple string replace() call for the output is acceptable.

Deciding How Many Event Handlers

The number of request handlers depends on the complexity of the page or the application. The implementation is up to the programmer and depends on a large number of objective and subjective criteria. If the GET and POST requests worked on different aspects of the application, their handlers could be implemented independently of one another like in Listing 2-4.

Listing 2-4. Independent Handlers for GET and POST Requests

```
class MainPage(webapp.RequestHandler):
  def get(self):
    self.response.out.write(mainForm())

class UserRequestHandler(webapp.RequestHandler):
```

```
   .
   .
   def post(self):
     output   = self.response.out
     baseWord = cgi.escape(
         self.request.get('baseWord'))
     password = self.__process(baseWord)
     output.write(mainForm().replace(
         "n/a", password))
```

Then request handlers must be specified in the applications instantiation tuple, as shown in Listing 2-5.

Listing 2-5. Multiple Request Handlers in Definitions for the Application

```
def main():
  application = webapp.WSGIApplication(
      [
        ('/', MainPage),
        ('/passwordGenRequest', UserRequestHandler)
      ], debug=True)
  run_wsgi_app(application)
```

The mappings are defined as URL-to-handler objects. The RequestHander class is defined in the webapp and must be the superclass of any concrete HTTP request handler, like those defined in Listing 2-4. The URL invoked from the browser determines which handler will execute:

```
<form method='POST' action='/passwordGenRequest'>
```

The logical grouping of request handlers is up to the implementer.

Debugging the Application

The App Engine troubleshooting tools are limited to using the debugging features in the development web server, the WSGIApplication objects' configuration, and displaying inline data in the application's output.

Debugging Options for the Development Web Server

The development server's default output goes to the console, where it can be piped, redirected, or visually inspected. Users control its debugging behavior through the command line options in Table 2-1.

Table 2-1. Development Web Server Debugging Options

OPTION	DESCRIPTION
`--debug`	Shows verbose messages in the console
`--debug_imports`	Shows errors about Python module imports and search paths
`--history_path`	Saves the local datastore change log for later inspection (see Chapter 7)

Debugging a WSGIApplication

The `WSGIApplication` class takes two parameters, as shown earlier in this chapter:

```
class WSGIApplication(locatorMapping, debug=False)
```

Toggle the `debug` argument to `True` when instantiating the `WSGIApplication` object to generate debugging information to the web browser. Each `RequestHandler` object defines a `handle_exception()` method that gets called when the handler raises an exception.

Unless the handler is overridden by the application's concrete implementations of `RequestHandler`, it will print a plain error message and set the HTTP status code to 500 (server error) before returning. If `debug=True` in the application instance, the handler will also send a stack trace to the web browser. Implementers may define custom behavior by overriding this method.

Implementing a Debugging Aid

The debugging options for the development server and the
WSGIApplication objects aren't sufficient for troubleshooting application
behavior, so writing a debugging aid may be a good option for some
applications. Such an aid could be used for including runtime request status
or custom information about the request handler state, cookies, headers, or
other application objects in the application's web page output. Figure 2-2
shows the class hierarchy for such a tool.

Figure 2-2. DDTHandler debugging aid component hierarchy

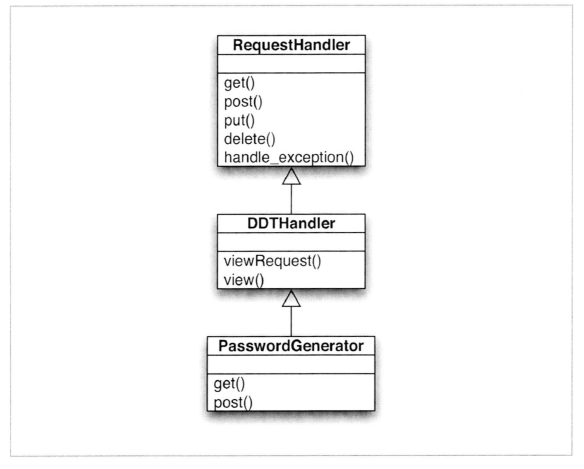

The request handlers would implement the DDTHandler instead of the RequestHandler from webapp framework, with an implementation like the one in Listing 2-6. This implementation uses inheritance instead of aggregation, because access to the member objects and methods in RequestHandler is automatic and less verbose than passing or reflecting them from a member object.

Listing 2-6. ddt.py

```python
#!/usr/bin/python

import cgi
import wsgiref.handlers

from google.appengine.ext import webapp

class DDTHandler(webapp.RequestHandler):

  def __startDisplay(self):
    self.response.out.write("<!--\n")

  def __endDisplay(self):
    self.response.out.write("-->\n")

  def __showDictionaryItems(self, dictionary, title):
    if (len(dictionary) > 0):
      request = self.request
      out      = self.response.out
      out.write("\n"+title+":\n")
      for key, value in dictionary.iteritems():
        out.write(key+" = "+value+"\n")

  def __showRequestMembers(self):
    request = self.request
    out      = self.response.out

    out.write(request.url+"\n")
```

```
    out.write("Query = "+request.query_string+"\n")
    out.write("Remote = "+request.remote_addr+"\n")
    out.write("Path = "+request.path+"\n\n")
    out.write("Request payload:\n")
    if (len(request.arguments()) > 0):
      for argument in request.arguments():
        value = cgi.escape(request.get(argument))
        out.write(argument+" = "+value+"\n")
    else:
      out.write("Empty\n")
    self.__showDictionaryItems(
        request.headers, "Headers")
    self.__showDictionaryItems(
        request.cookies, "Cookies")

  def viewRequest(self):
    self.__startDisplay()
    self.__showRequestMembers()
    self.__endDisplay()

  def view(self, aString):
    self.__startDisplay()
    self.response.out.write(aString+"\n")
    self.__endDisplay()
```

The output is sent to the client in the form of embedded comments viewable in the HTML source. Listing 2-7 shows that the classes using such a feature implement DDTHandler instead of the webapp RequestHandler, and the implementer may call its methods from anywhere in the code.

Listing 2-7. Changes to passwordgenerator.py

```
.
.
class PasswordGenerator(DDTHandler):

  def get(self):
```

```
      self.viewRequest()
      self.response.out.write(mainForm())

   def post(self):
      self.viewRequest()
      output    = self.response.out
   .
   .
```

DDTHandler users may also view arbitrary strings by invoking

```
   self.view("Some string here")
```

Listing 2-8 is the sample output for the request handlers in the GenPasswd application.

Listing 2-8. Sample Output from DDTHandler Calls

```
<!--
http://localhost:8080/
Query =
Remote = 127.0.0.1
Path = /

Request payload:
baseWord = ThisisTheSecretword
-->
<html>
.
.
<!-- Some string here! -->
.
.
</html>
```

The main disadvantage of this method is that output must wait until a successful response, along with the rest of the data, returns from the server. Its advantage comes in play with the ability to view the internal application state even when the code is pushed to the hosted Google App Engine.

Interactive Debugging

The sandbox limitations imposed by the development web server and Google App Engine prevent use of the `pdb` module. Although `import pdb` will work without problems, attempts at execution traces will throw an exception and kill the executing program, along with displaying a nasty traceback page on the browser.

Developers may debug pure Python code outside of the App Engine's environment in a standard Python console and then merge it with the application. More sophisticated debugging tools are also available from several open source and commercial tool providers.

ECLIPSE AND PYDEV

PyDev is an Eclipse plug-in for Python development that supports such interactive debugging features as breakpoints and watchpoints, stepping in, out, and over code, and so on. It also comes with full IDE capabilities for Python 2.5 or later, a console view, and code formatter. The package requires Eclipse 3.2 or later and is available from `http://pydev.sourceforge.net`.

Publishing to the Web

Publishing to the Web is a simple process, but it requires a modicum of planning. There are a few considerations prior to actually uploading the files to the server:

- Each application gets a unique ID; neither the application nor the ID may be removed from Google Apps once they've been defined.

- A limited number of applications may be defined per registered account until the Google App Engine preview ends; the original number was three, then it was bumped up to nine and to higher counts later, but this number isn't infinite.

- Applications may be updated at any time, but the only way to disable an application, since it can't be removed, is by uploading a blank `app.yaml` configuration file.

- Google's given no word about when the preview program will end, so planning commercial deployments of multiple applications is not an option for the time being.

Creating and Registering an Application

Follow these steps to create and register your application:

1. Go to `http://appengine.google.com`.

2. The first page shows an empty list of My Applications. Click the Create an Application button.

3. Enter the unique application identifier and other relevant information, as shown in Figure 2-3. Although most of the options are self-explanatory, the authentication options require a bit of planning.

Figure 2-3. Registering an application with Google App Engine

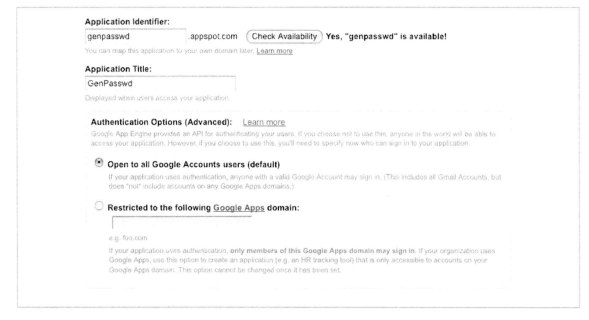

Applications can be either public or restricted to the Google App domain. Open-to-all applications are general-purpose applications, like GenPasswd, intended for use by anyone with a Google or Gmail account. Restricted applications are limited to users registered with the Google Apps domain. Companies using Google Apps may need to keep user access to those in their own domains, hence the separation. Once an application is registered, though, the authentication mechanism cannot be changed. The authentication mechanisms are discussed in Chapter 5.

Uploading an Application

The unique application identifier is used for locating the application on the Web as well as within the Google App Engine runtime. Setting up the application ID in the `app.yaml` configuration file is the last required step for publishing if the application was created successfully. Edit the `app.yaml` file, and ensure that the `application:` tag has the same application ID that you defined in the Google Apps setup.

Use the `appcfg.py` tools to upload the app to Google Apps. The command sequence used for uploading the GenPasswd tools follows:

```
appcfg.py --no_cookies update genpasswd/
```

`appcfg.py` tools uses the Google App credentials for transferring the application files. The `--no_cookies` switch tells the tool to not store the authentication information; if the switch is not used, `appcfg.py` will just upload the files without asking for credentials on every subsequent call.

If the upload was successful, point a web browser at the URL `[applicationid].appspot.com` (replace `applicationid` with the actual application identifier) to see your application run, as in Figure 2-4.

Figure 2-4. An application running on Google Apps

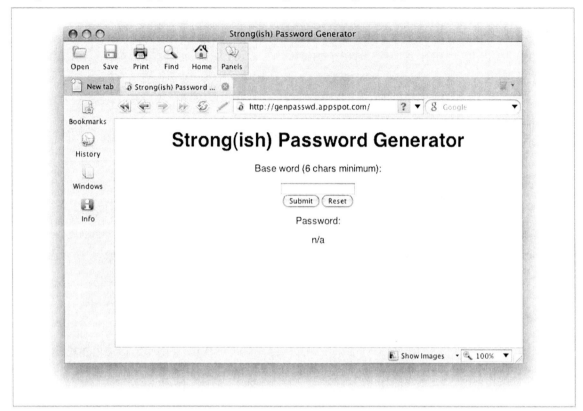

Running an Application from a Custom Domain

Follow these steps to configure an application to run from your custom domain:

1. Log on to `http://appengine.google.com`.

2. Select the application for the custom domain name; this will go to the Dashboard.

3. Select Versions.

4. Click Add a Domain.

5. Enter the domain name where the application will live (e.g., eugeneciurana.com). Sign up with Google Apps to prove domain ownership.

6. If Google Apps isn't aware of this domain yet, sign up for the service by going to http://www.google.com/apps. Follow the instructions from Google to register the new domain with them.

7. Read and accept the terms of service and confirm the application's web address (e.g., getpasswd.eugeneciurana.com)

8. Set the CNAME record for the application to point at ghs.google.com (e.g., genpasswd CNAME ghs.google.com) in your domain name server (DNS) and confirm the change in the Google Apps page; Listing 2-9 shows the sample record for GenPasswd. Consult with the hosting provider or system administrator in your organization to set up the CNAME record if you aren't familiar with DNS configuration.

Listing 2-9. Sample DNS Configuration for GenPasswd

```
$TTL 3D
@   IN SOA varenka.eugeneciurana.com. \
    hostmaster.eugeneciurana.com. (
                        1170720946
                        8H
                        2H
                        4W
                        1D )
NS          varenka
            MX          10 varenka
            MX          20 lavender
localhost   A           127.0.0.1
@           A           74.0.125.28
lavender    A           74.0.125.26
varenka     A           74.0.125.28
            MX          10 varenka
            MX          20 lavender
www         CNAME       varenka
genpasswd   CNAME       ghs.google.com.
```

Google defines the `ghs.google.com` IP address. If you define this record in your own servers, don't forget the trailing period at the end of the CNAME definition, since it tells your DNS server to get its IP address from the Google DNS server. Your system administrator or hosting provider can help you in setting this up if you aren't familiar with the intricacies name server configuration.

Summary

This chapter covered all the steps involved in deploying a new application from start to publishing and warned about a few of the gotchas for each. The sample application was contrived to showcase each of these steps. A real application often requires better ways of interacting with the end user, robust authentication, the ability to store data, and interaction with other applications.

How is Google App Engine designed to take advantage of available features? We'll explore that in Chapter 3.

Chapter 3: The Design of a Google App Engine Application

Chapters 1 and 2 provided an introduction to the App Engine concepts and tools but didn't quite deal with application design and implementation. The rest of this book will focus on how to develop complete applications using the API features and how to manage the application once it's been published.

A web-based application on the cloud deals with more than just web pages. It must provide account slots and session management for different users, handle persistence, and perhaps interact with other systems through web services or other conduits. This chapter discusses the design process based on a simple application.

The BookmarksBin Application

Everyone using a web browser sooner or later needs to manage bookmarks. Some people prefer the bookmark lists built into their browsers. Others prefer bookmarking sites like delicious, and others use both. The rest of this book will discuss the design and implementation of the BookmarksBin application. Providing bookmark management and global access are its main design goals. It doesn't provide the social networking aspects of tagging or bookmarking sites like Technorati or delicious.

The Data Model

BookmarksBin will track two kinds of objects: URLs and tags. It will use tags for grouping results instead creating topical folders, like the bookmarks grouping offered by web browsers. Users will have the option of managing the tags and the bookmarks lists. The data model in Figure 3-1 shows these basic tables and their columns and the mechanisms for associating both.

Figure 3-1. The BookmarksBin data model

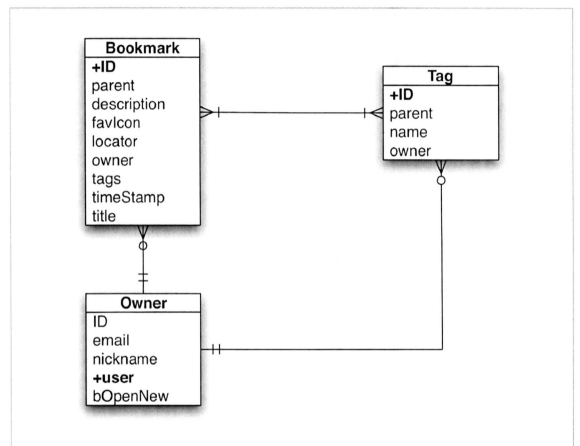

The owner entity has a unique ID because Google Accounts doesn't guarantee the uniqueness of its two main attributes: user nickname and user e-mail address. Users may be able to switch e-mail addresses in the future, and user-specific data needs to be associated with the account somehow. The e-mail account switch should be handled independently of applications that associate an owner with one or more data sets.

Wait, No User Table?

Web applications rely on some kind of user registration and authentication system. Implementations may use any of these approaches to solve that problem:

- Create a database schema and the API and services to use it from various applications.

- Use Active Directory or LDAP to manage users and roles and provide authentication through a single sign-on system that abstracts the providers.

- Delegate the registration and authentication scheme to a third party, and then use API or web services and authentication tokens to manage users.

App Engine provides services for implementing user registration and authentication through its Users API. App Engine applications don't need to implement this logic, because they delegate authentication and session initialization to Google Accounts. The upside is that Google has already implemented all the grunt work, and App Engine applications can use the same authentication mechanisms as Gmail, Google Calendar, or iGoogle. The downside is that users must have at least a Gmail account if they wish to use App Engine applications that require authentication.

Session authentication and account registration will be discussed in Chapter 5.

Web Application Architecture

BookmarksBin appears to users as a list where bookmarks can be added, changed, or deleted. Users must log on to the application to gain access to account bookmarks. Figure 3-2 shows the basic navigation flow for the site.

Figure 3-2. The BookmarksBin application architecture

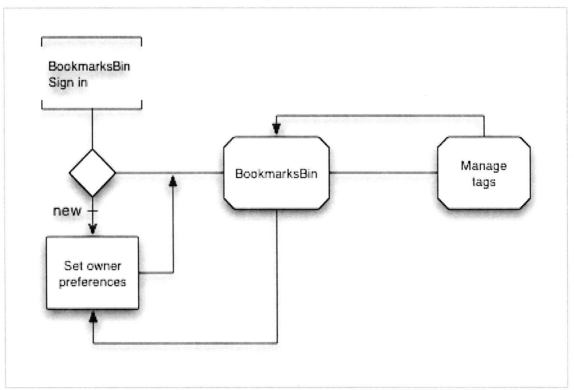

The App Engine infrastructure and the User object handle application sign in. Navigation depends on establishing a successful session with the application, and the application container manages session-specific information in tandem with the owner data described in the data model.

There are three basic application components: the BookmarksBin core, the tags manager, and a page for setting user preferences. Users navigate to the other page sets in the system to perform ancillary tasks but always end up in the BookmarksBin main page upon completion of those tasks.

Figure 3-3 shows the pages associated with the BookmarksBin application. The user is using the bookmarks to link to other locations, searching for bookmarks, and deleting or modifying the attributes of a specific bookmark.

Figure 3-3. The BookmarksBin component

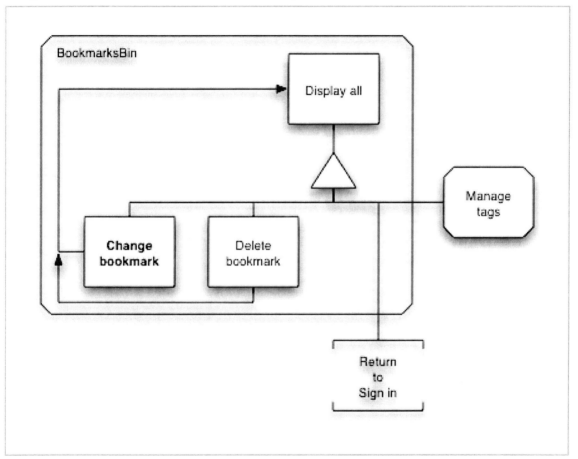

Tags associated with bookmarks are the main classification method. The user may arrange which bookmarks are displayed by selecting one or more tags; a bookmark can have at least one tag, or it can be unclassified. The unclassified tag is used for any page that doesn't have any other tags.

Figure 3-4 shows the tag management component and the pages associated with it. The user can display all of them and add or remove tags. The UI portion of the tag is responsible for ensuring that no duplicate tags exist, and it displays the number of bookmarks associated with a specific tag.

Figure 3-4. The tags manager

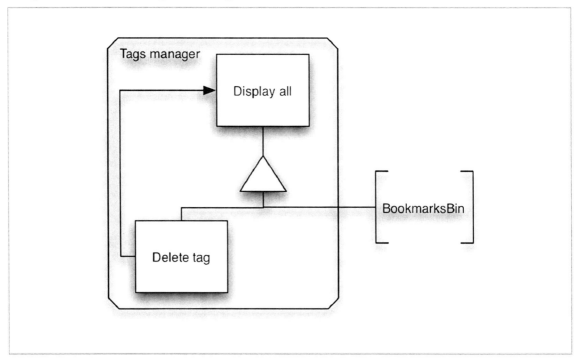

Pages-to-Components Mapping

Chapter 2 pointed out that an application may have one or more request handlers, and each request handler may refer to multiple pages. BookmarksBin will define three request handlers for the application itself, the tags manager, and the user preferences page. Each will have one or more views associated with it as either static pages or templates where content will be displayed.

Summary

This chapter described what the BookmarksBin application internals are like so that they can be implemented with the Google App Engine API. With that in mind, let's begin writing our application in the next chapter.

Chapter 4: Building an Application

The previous chapters laid the foundation for starting, writing, and deploying applications for Google App Engine. This chapter is about how to lay out the web pages for the application, how to use webapp and other frameworks, and how to deal with dynamic content, static files, page formatting, and JavaScript in the context of the application.

The BookmarksBin needs a user interface that uses the features relevant to a modern web application. This chapter provides the basics for building its user interface by leveraging the webapp Framework and others.

Working with the webapp Framework

The webapp Framework is a powerful-but-simple application tool set. It's the easiest way to write applications for App Engine by providing enough features to get the job done condensed in a simple and elegant API.

The webapp API provides these services to application developers:

- HTTP 1.1 request handlers
- Mechanisms for manipulating data within the framework's context
- A WSGI-compatible interface
- Tools for handling response headers, status codes, or redirects
- A templating engine

The templating engine and how to combine it with static files and in-page scripting are our focus for building applications, since the request handling basics were already covered in Chapter 2.

Mixing any combination of HTML, cascading style sheets (CSS), JavaScript, and Python is always a bad idea because it ends in maintenance nightmares. This style of coding also produces brittle, hard-to-modularize code and redundant classes and functions. Listing 2-3 shows a poor man's template built into the main Python listing, logically separated from the main program's business logic but still requiring mixing Python and string processing to generate the program's output. This was OK for a simple example but isn't acceptable for a more complex application.

Templates are used for separating the presentation aspects of the application from its business logic. The template engine combines data provided by the application with one or more templates to produce a coherent view of the data, as shown in Figure 4-1.

Figure 4-1. HTML generation from templates

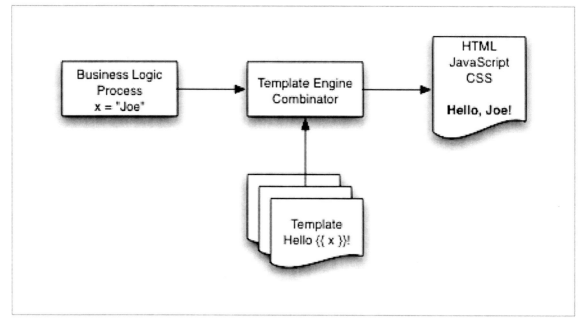

The template engine is responsible for resolving variables defined in special tags in the template using data provided by the application; in this case, variable x has the user's name and replaces its reference {{x}} in the output to generate a friendly, "Hello, Joe!" message. Templates can deal with individual data tags or iterate through complex sets, separating the presentation logic from the application's business logic. Last, templates also allow better component reusability, whether dealing with whole pages or with subelements within a page, like headers or navigation bars. The BookmarksBin user interface is entirely based on templates.

Working With Other Frameworks

The webapp Framework is the default tool set for building web applications but not the only one. App Engine supports any WSGI-compatible framework as long as it's written entirely in Python.

webapp and its template-resolution features center around a simple request/response/dispatch model. Full-stack application frameworks offer more robust features for the more experienced web application developers. The only caveat is that some of those features may be unavailable out of the box due to App Engine's sandbox restrictions.

Django is one of the most complete Python frameworks (in fact, webapp uses some of its features like the templating engine) and has been integrated to run in App Engine, though work continues to provide a full feature set. There are at least two framework-porting projects, like the google-app-engine-django project and Gaengo, a forked reimplementation intended to run exclusively on App Engine. Other frameworks are being ported all the time, but the list is too long and volatile to reproduce here.

Tip   Checking the Google Groups discussion boards is the best way to find out if App Engine supports a specific web application framework: `http://groups.google.com/group/google-appengine/topics`.

Installing a more robust web application framework will provide more advanced features like URL dispatching and context processors that webapp doesn't provide. Just be ready to ship the framework along with the rest of the application when it's published and to modify any functions or objects that conflict with the App Engine sandbox rules.

Laying Out Applications with webapp Templates

Figure 4-2 shows the application layout for BookmarksBin. The application pages have a combination of common elements, like the header and footer, and content generated in context with an application activity.

Figure 4-2. BookmarksBin application layout

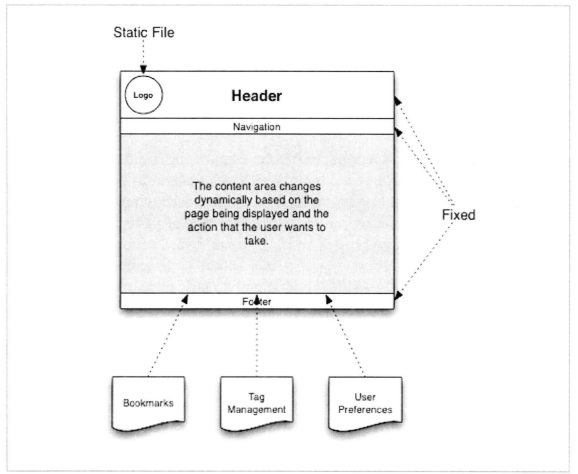

The fixed portions of the page are good candidates for reuse across all pages in the application, leaving each request handler to populate the content of its context-specific pages.

Exploring the Template Hierarchy

webapp's templating engine is really a version of Django's; App Engine provides only minimal documentation for it so it's helpful to open a copy of the Django reference guide in a web browser during development.

Caution   The templating engine in webapp at the time of this writing is based on Django version 0.96. The Django framework has released other versions since, so ensure that the documentation that you consult matches the release in webapp. The current information about which template engine version to use for reference is available from `http://code.google.com/appengine/docs/gettingstarted/templates.html`.

---

webapp and Django templates support inheritance and aggregation for development. Listing 4-1 shows the basic template used by all pages of the BookmarksBin application and shows various `<div>` sections corresponding to the page elements depicted in Figure 4-2.

Listing 4-1. The bookmarksbinpage.html Ancestor Template

```html
<html>
  <head>
    <title>
      {% block title %}
        If you see this, your page is incomplete
      {% endblock title %}
    </title>
  </head>

  <body>
    <!-- common header for all pages -->
    <div id="header">
      <h1>BookmarksBin</h1>
    </div>
```

```
<div id="navigation">
    {% include "navigation.html" %}
</div>

<div id="content">
    {% block content %}
    {% endblock content %}
</div>

<!-- common fooger -->
<div id="footer">
</div>
  </body>
</html>
```

The navigation menu is aggregated into the template using the `{% include %}` statement, and it's implemented as a stand-alone snippet that will be inserted at that inclusion point in the code (see Listing 4-2).

Listing 4-2. navigation.html

```
<ul>
    <li>Main</li>
    <li>Tags</li>
    <li>Preferences</li>
</ul>
```

Assembling the Templates and Handlers

Listing 4-3 shows the first implementation of the `bookmarksbin.html` page depicting where most of the elements will be in the final version of the program.

Listing 4-3. bookmarksbin.html

```
{% extends "bookmarksbinpage.html" %}

{% block title %}BookmarksBin{% endblock %}
```

```
{% block content %}
  <h2>My Bookmarks</h2>

  <table id="bookmarksTable">
    {% for bookmark in bookmarks %}
      <tr id="{% cycle evenRow,oddRow %}">
        <td style="width: 15%;">
          {{bookmark.timeStamp}}
        </td>
        <td>
          {{bookmark.icon}}
          <a href="{{bookmark.url}}" target="_new" />
            {{bookmark.title}}
          </a><br>
          {{bookmark.description}}
        </td>
      </tr>
    {% endfor %}
  </table>
{% endblock %}
```

The body of this main page includes only template elements that are unique to it in well defined blocks that will be replaced in the parent at the same block locations defined in Listing 4-1. The blocks in the child override the same block definitions in the ancestor template.

The result of integrating the templates and Python request handlers is the web page shown in Figure 4-3. The page generated by Listing 4-3 will display bookmarks from a persistent list managed by the application.

Figure 4-3. The basic BookmarksBin main page

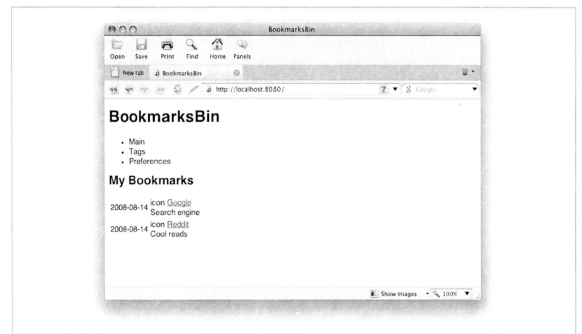

The template's code iterates through a static list, as defined in Listing 4-4.

Listing 4-4. bookmarksbin.py (partial)

```
bookmarks = [
  Bookmark(
      date.today(), 'icon', 'Search engine',
      'http://www.google.com', 'Google'),
  Bookmark(
      date.today(), 'icon', 'Cool reads',
      'http://www.reddit.com', 'Reddit')
]
.
class BookmarksBin(AppHandler):
  def __displayBookmarksPage(self):
    x = {
        'bookmarks': bookmarks }
    self.renderPage('bookmarksbin.html', x)
```

```
def get(self):
    if self.hasValidUser():
        self.__displayBookmarksPage()
```

The static list is a collection of bookmark objects. `bookmarksbin.html` is concerned only with a bookmark's creation time, the site's favicon, a user-provided description, the site's URL, and its title. The complete object, its associated data model, and its related operations are described in Chapter 6.

Since the application will host multiple users, it also checks if a valid user is logged in and forces a credentials exchange if that's not the case. User validation mechanisms will be discussed in Chapter 5. Figure 4-4 shows the class hierarchy for the BookmarsBin components.

Figure 4-4. The BookmarksBin class hierarchy

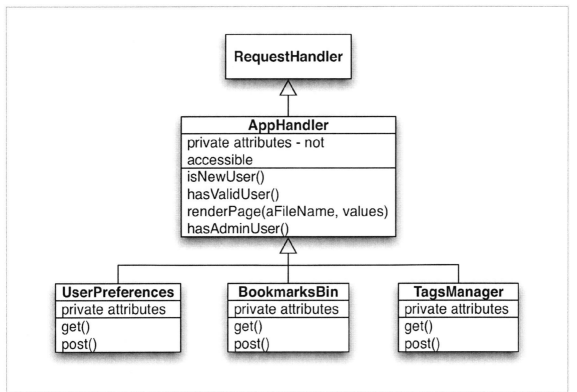

All the request handlers implement the same mechanisms for signing in or validating a user, establishing if the user is new to the system, and they render the pages associated with each event handler. The rendering method in Listing 4-5 accepts the template file name and the substitution variables.

Listing 4-5. The renderPage() Method

```
from google.appengine.ext.webapp import template
.
def renderPage(self, fileName, values):
    path = os.path.join(os.path.dirname(__file__),
        fileName)
    self.response.out.write(
        template.render(path, values))
```

The sandbox rules allow file input from the file system. This method reads the template from a directory accessible through the application's home directory (i.e., the one defined in App Launcher or manually) and passes the values list to the `template.render()` method from webapp. All these operations could be done in-line in the handler's `get()` or `post()` method, but that would lead to repetitious code among every handler.

The `values` variable contains a dictionary of objects. For each entry, the key corresponds to an identifier used in the template, and the value matches to the object that will be replaced in the named template variable. This relationship is defined in Figure 4-5. The values can be any valid Python objects and may be substituted directly by querying each individual value or by iterating through its elements if the value is a sequence data type (as defined in the *Python Library Reference*, section 3.6). In this example, the `values` variable contains a dictionary with only one entry, `bookmarks`, which contains a list of `Bookmark` objects defined in Listing 4-4.

A modern web application consists of dynamically generated files, images, JavaScript, CSS, and other static files. Generating everything from templates would be cumbersome, would tax App Engine's infrastructure for no good reason by forcing extra execution cycles, and would be somewhat hard to manage. The next sections discuss how to implement static content and client-side programming in combination with an application's request handlers.

Figure 4-5. The relationship between template variables and values

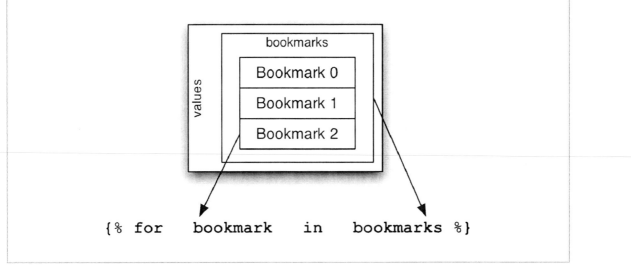

Using Static Files

Static files may account for a significant part of the application. App Engine is designed to not serve static files on request, the way a regular web server would.

App Engine will serve specific files and bypass handlers only if the directory where they are located is defined as a static path in the app.yaml file like in Listing 4-6.

Listing 4-6. Defining Static Paths in app.yaml

```
handlers:
- url: /images
  static_dir: images
```

```
 - url: /styles
   static_dir: css

 - url: /scripts
   static_dir: scripts

 - url: .*
   script: bookmarksbin.py
```

Caution   Keep in mind that the `url:` definition is a *regular expression*, not a directory name or file system pattern. If a definition like `url: .*` appears in the handlers section before the URL definitions like `/name` for `static_dir` handlers, any request for that static content will fail and return a 404 error code.

These patterns can be used for referencing or linking static files from the rendered HTML or to serve user requests. A request including the `/images` pattern will first match the pattern itself and then append the rest of the path before serving the file if present or throwing a 404 error. A reference to an application logo file, for example, is implemented like in Listing 4-7.

Listing 4-7. Using Static Content from a Template or Static HTML File

```
<img src="/images/BookmarksBin-logo.gif"
         border="0" width="40" height="40"
         align="left" />
```

Notice that the static file path must match the definition in the `app.yaml` file. The file locations aren't relative paths like in a traditional web server. The `url:` definitions represent specific patterns that must be matched, the `static_dir:` or `static_files:` directives tell the server where the content lives in the file system, relative to the application's virtual home directory.

THE APP.YAML STATIC FILE-HANDLING DIRECTIVES

`app.yaml` offers the `static_dir:` directive for handling every file in an application subdirectory and the `static_files:` directive for handling specific files or file patterns. Files found in the application's directory that aren't static are considered application or data files and are uploaded during updates to the Google Apps servers.

`app.yaml` also has a directive called `skip_files:` that uses regular expressions for specifying which files in the application home directory are not to be uploaded to App Engine.

The `app.yaml` reference guide has the complete list of static file handling directives and can be found here:

`http://code.google.com/appengine/docs/`
`configuringanapp.html`

Displaying a Favicon

Every successful web browser request to the development server triggers at least two log messages:

```
"GET / HTTP/1.1" 200 -
"GET /favicon.ico HTTP/1.1" 404 -
```

The first request serves the home page for the application; the second one is a request for serving a favicon graphic; that's the tiny icon that browsers display in the address bar next to a page's URL or along with its bookmark. Setting up a handler for serving a `favicon.ico` file is simple. First, update the `app.yaml` file as shown in Listing 4-8.

Listing 4-8. Serving a Specific Static File Configuration

```
- url: /favicon\.ico
  static_files: favicon.ico
  upload: favicon\.ico
```

The `upload:` directive is used for specifying which files must be uploaded to App Engine during an update, because they are uploaded and handled separately from the application and data files. Defining only the `static_files:` directive without `upload:` results in a runtime error when trying to run the application.

Finally, update the `bookmarksbinpage.html` abstract template to include an explicit reference to the `favincon.ico` file and its location in the `<head>` section:

```
<link rel="shortcut icon" href="/favicon.ico"
    type="image/x-icon" />
```

The icon will be available from the application's home directory whenever any of its pages are loaded, as shown in Figure 4-6.

Figure 4-6. The application displays static graphics and icon files

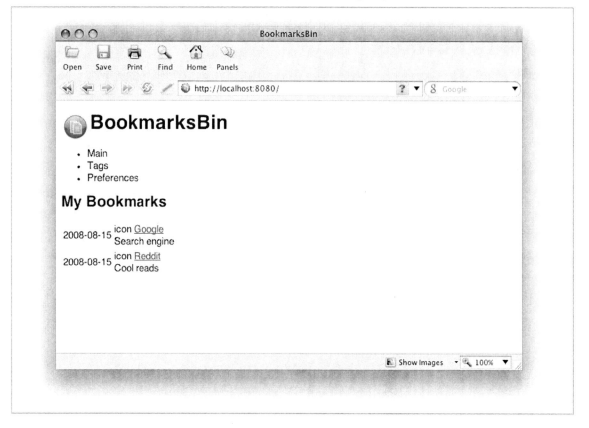

Beautifying Your User Interface with CSS

Support for CSS is straightforward. Like with any other static file, first define the url: expression in a request for finding the file, and then place the CSS files in the appropriate directory off the application's root. Figure 4-7 shows that the page now uses a different font.

Figure 4-7. CSS applied to the BookmarksBin sample page

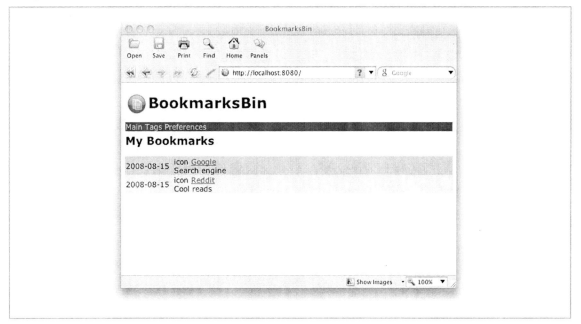

The foundations of the interactive user interface have been laid out for the navigation bar. After defining the CSS file, adding this tag to the `bookmarksbinpage.html` abstract template's `<head>` section was the only change needed to apply the styles:

```
<link rel="stylesheet" type="text/css"
    href="/styles/bookmarksbin.css" />
```

Remember to include the leading slash (/) for the static directory name, or the file won't resolve correctly.

Downloading the Source Files for the Examples

All the source files, including images and others, are available for download from `http://bookmarksbin.appspot.com/sources` or the Apress web site.

The examples are too long to include in this chapter except where the complete file is necessary for explaining a concept. From now until the end of the book, all examples will show only the snippets relevant to explaining a specific concept and where the snippet fits in the context of the application. The complete source files will be served as static content as described in this section.

Summary

The visual and interactive aspects of an application combine dynamic and static event handlers, templates, Python code, and configuration file modifications. Orchestrating them isn't hard, but remember the App Engine rules for working with each of them so that the client browsers render them correctly.

Now that we've covered the basics of defining the UI, how do we begin to make it interactive? How do we go about granting user access to the application? Chapter 5 describes how to manage users and their access to the application.

Chapter 5: What About the Users?

Applications must have some way of authenticating users. Authentication is just the process of validating that a user has access to the resources that the application provides. Credentials exchange is the most common authentication mechanism.

Regular applications rely on authentication schemes like these:

- *Operating system user account*: The operating system grants access and privileges based on its own user definitions or based on an access control list (ACL) that matches users or user groups against a domain's permissions.

- *Framework authentication*: The application framework provides an API, the facilities for implementing a users master database, and the calls for validating credentials against this database.

- *Single sign-on authentication*: The application uses a network-based API that allows multiple applications to use the same authentication mechanism. Users use the same credentials for all the applications in the group, and sometimes, the applications automatically authenticate a user after successful authentication across more two or more systems during a single work session within the same domain.

The App Engine user API is a combination of framework and single sign-on authentication schemes. It relies on Google's sign-in for authentication and provides a Python API for using its services.

This chapter shows how to add the App Engine's authentication services to an application, how to use user objects, and the relationship between application authentication and the datastore.

Authentication and Google Accounts

App Engine users, for the most part, can't do much without a valid Google account. Most nontrivial applications will store data associated with specific users, using the user's Google account. Google accounts are almost always tied to the user's Gmail account, so they're easy to remember.

Note   App Engine user accounts are unique. At the time of this writing, the user's e-mail account is the only key, though the documentation indicates that this may change in the future.

These are the advantages of using a Google account:

- The application automatically redirects users to the Google accounts registration or sign-in before allowing access to its resources.

- Assuming that the user already has a Google account, signing on to the application is just a matter of using the same credentials as for other Google properties; new users don't need to create a new account.

- Application developers don't need to worry about creating a login system or about how to tie it to the user application preferences mechanism.

- Applications can detect if a user is an administrator based on its App Engine settings, simplifying application flow.

This coupling may result in App Engine applications appearing on a user's Google Accounts page in the future. Providing developers with a mechanism for accessing the user's data without handling the user's login information is the main design goal. This allows for enhanced application security and a simpler, standardized authentication mechanism for all Google applications.

Using GData Services

The Google Data API (GData) provides a simple protocol for exchanging data between web applications over the RSS or Atom formats. GData is implemented through the Representational State Transfer (REST) protocol open to any application or device that can use HTTP 1.1 and its basic API. It provides a general model for feeds, queries, and results.

Tip   Learn the fundamentals of REST at `http://en.wikipedia.org/wiki/Representational_State_Transfer`.

GData is relevant because App Engine applications can use the API for interacting with other Google properties, such as these:

- Authentication
- Google Base
- Calendar
- Documents
- Picasa Web Albums
- YouTube

This chapter covers GData usage, because it's tied to user authentication and the Users API.

Note   There is more information about GData at `http://code.google.com/apis/gdata/`.

User Objects

User objects correspond to a unique user with a Google account. Uniqueness is enforced within the App Engine and the Google ecosystem; instances are comparable and unique. Whenever two instances are equal, they are guaranteed to refer to the same user.

User instances are simple objects. The only attributes that they handle are the user's nickname and the e-mail address, as shown in Figure 5-1.

Figure 5-1. User instance attributes

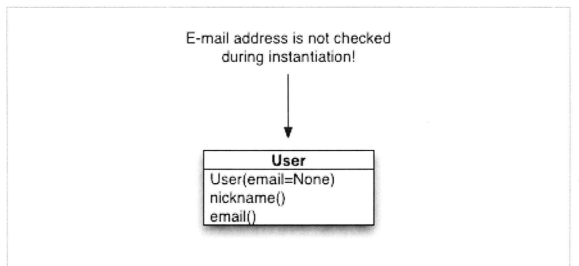

A user object must include an e-mail address when instanced. Developers must be careful to use only e-mail addresses associated with a valid Google account; the system supports them but doesn't enforce their use. As a result, it's entirely possible to crate a brand new user with a bogus, non-Google Accounts address that will never match a real user.

Valid Google Accounts credentials may be tied to any Google service that supports them, including Gmail accounts. This excludes all Google Apps domain accounts, though this may change in the future.

What About Specific Domains?

Access control to an application would be very coarse if any user with a valid account could use it. How would you control access to users associated with a specific domain?

Let's address the good news first: access control can be limited through the use of domains registered with Google Apps. If such a domain exists, any of its members may access the application, and nobody else. The application will be available only through its subdomain name, as described in Chapter 2. Access control is granted by administering the users in that Google Apps domain.

The bad news is that custom domains and custom authentication options can only be set during initial application upload and configuration with Google Apps, like in Figure 5-2.

Figure 5-2. User authentication options during setup

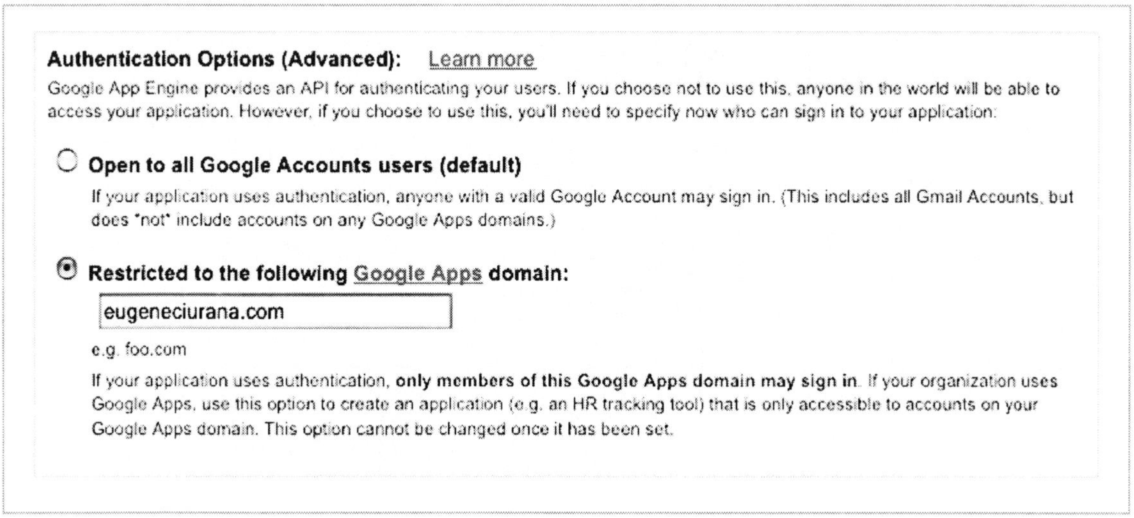

Authentication Options (Advanced): Learn more

Google App Engine provides an API for authenticating your users. If you choose not to use this, anyone in the world will be able to access your application. However, if you choose to use this, you'll need to specify now who can sign in to your application:

○ **Open to all Google Accounts users (default)**

    If your application uses authentication, anyone with a valid Google Account may sign in. (This includes all Gmail Accounts, but does "not" include accounts on any Google Apps domains.)

◉ **Restricted to the following Google Apps domain:**

    `eugeneciurana.com`

    e.g. foo.com

    If your application uses authentication, **only members of this Google Apps domain may sign in.** If your organization uses Google Apps, use this option to create an application (e.g. an HR tracking tool) that is only accessible to accounts on your Google Apps domain. This option cannot be changed once it has been set.

Getting a Valid User Object and the Users API

So now you're asking yourself, "How can I get a valid User object for my application?" You simply ask Google Accounts to provide you with one by using the sequence of API calls shown in Figure 5-3.

Figure 5-3. Getting a valid user for the application

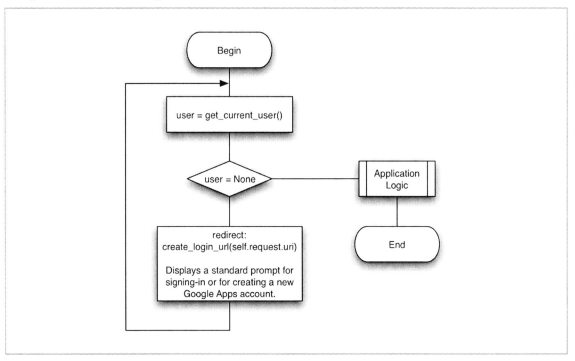

Listing 5-1 shows how the BookmarksBin application authenticates users, implementing the flow from Figure 5-3. AppHandler is a superclass for all objects that make the BookmarksBin application, as described in Figure 4-4.

Listing 5-1. AppHandler Class Basic Implementation

```python
#!/usr/bin/python

import os

from google.appengine.api import users
from google.appengine.ext.webapp import RequestHandler
from google.appengine.ext.webapp import template

class AppHandler(RequestHandler):
  # *** Private members ***

  # *** Public members ***

def hasValidUser(self):
    self._user = users.get_current_user()

    if self._user:
      if self.isNewUser():
        self.__setUserPreferences()
      return True
    else:
      self.redirect(users.create_login_url(
          self.request.uri))
```

The get_current_user() function returns a valid user if one holds an application session; otherwise, it returns None. If no user is available, the handler executes create_login_url() using the target URL to display if the user successfully logs on using a Google account. All the event handlers can use the logic in Listing 5-2 to guarantee a valid user session before performing their tasks.

The Google sign-in page from Figure 5-4 won't allow a user to continue into the application unless that user has a valid account, as discussed earlier in this chapter.

Figure 5-4. Google sign-in for the BookmarksBin application

Other Users API Functions

There are two additional methods in the Users API:

- `create_logout_url(destination)`: Normally used in links, buttons, and page redirects, it returns a URL that allows the user to sign out and sends the user to a `destination` URL.

- `is_current_user_admin()`: It returns `True` when the current user is an application administrator defined in the application's dashboard.

Tip   The complete Users API documentation is available at `http://code.google.com/appengine/docs/users/`.

BROWSER PRIVACY OPTIONS AND COOKIE SETTINGS

Different browsers treat Google Accounts and Gmail account tokens in somewhat different ways when it comes to privacy options. Firefox and Safari, for example, proceed to the application without problems when the privacy options are set to allow cookies only from the site or domain where the current page originates, but not from third-party sites (like ad servers). Opera, however, is very strict on this regard: login will fail unless the user privacy options are set to accept all cookies and consider the Google Accounts site as different from `appspot.com`. Test authentication with as many browsers' privacy settings as possible to ensure an optimal user experience.

User Objects in the Datastore

Chapter 6 covers data persistence for an App Engine application in detail. This section discusses data persistence a bit too, because many applications require persisting user objects and preferences.

Figure 5-5 describes the relationship between the Datastore model and a user preferences class specific to the application. The selection of user preferences attributes is up to the application designer, but an attribute tying the user preferences object to the Google Accounts unique ID is mandatory.

Figure 5-5. UserPreferences class hierarchy

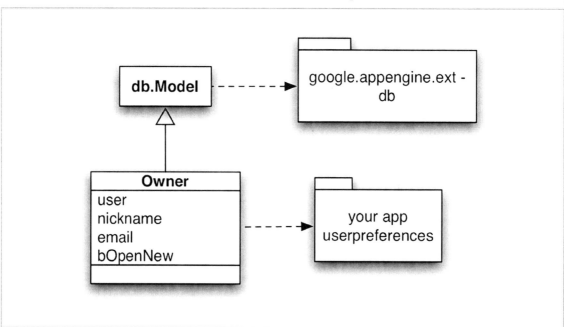

A basic `UserPreferences` class, like the one in Listing 5-2, defines its attributes in terms of the `Model` superclass. `Model` concrete implementations are typed, because the underlying Datastore (i.e., database) also carries typing information. Unlike with other Python objects, it's necessary to define each attribute's type so that instances can be stored and retrieved from the Datastore correctly.

The `UserPreferences` attribute types in Listing 5-2 don't represent an exhaustive list. This application needs to handle only a user's name, whether to sort the bookmarks by the date in which they were added or updated, and the mandatory user account reference.

Listing 5-2. userpreferences.py

```
from google.appengine.ext import db

class UserPreferences(db.Model):
    userName    = db.StringProperty()
    userAccount = db.UserProperty(required=True)
    bSortByDate = db.BooleanProperty()
```

An application may use the user preferences objects by invoking something like the code in Listing 5-3.

Listing 5-3. Sample UserPreferences Instantiation

```
from google.appengine.ext import users
from userpreferences import UserPreferences
.
currentUser = users.get_current_user()
if (currentUser):
    query = db.GqlQuery("SELECT * FROM UserPreferences
        WHERE userAccount = :1", currentUser)
    userPreferences = query.get()
    if (userPreferences != None):
      self._doSomethingWith(userPreferences)
```

The GQL query returns either `None` or a valid `UserPreferences` object. The query is bound to use the second parameter in the `currentUser` keyword. GQL is similar to SQL, but it diverges in how it treats some application-level objects like Google Apps accounts. This will be discussed in depth in the next chapter.

Configuring Admin Users

Some aspects of the application, like end-user management, Datastore maintenance, and runtime configuration, may require an administrator. For example, programmers may implement an administration console for the application and restrict access to the administrative functions to only some users.

Defining Admin Users

You may have guessed by now that administrative users are defined from your App Engine administration console, not from the application itself. Follow these steps to define an admin user:

1. Log on to `http://appengine.google.com`.

2. Select your application from the list ("bookmarksbin" for the examples in this chapter).

3. Select Developers under Administration.

4. Enter the e-mail address of the developers you want to invite to collaborate on this application, as shown in Figure 5-6.

Figure 5-6. Developers in a project are also application administrators.

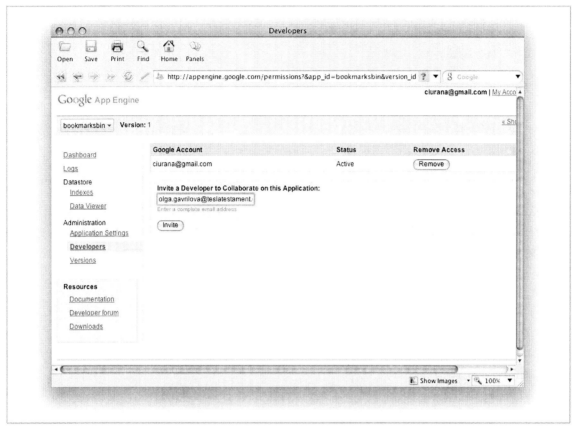

The developer will receive an invitation to collaborate in the application and will have access to this project administration console upon confirmation. The application will be able to query the developer's status as an administrator and offer additional functionality, if available.

Validating Admin Users in the Code

Admin user validation is quite simple: just call the
`is_current_user_admin()` function from the users package, as shown in
Listing 5-4.

Listing 5-4. Admin User Validation in the AppHandler Class

```
# From apptools.py
class AppHandler(RequestHandler):
    .
  def hasAdminUser(self):
    if self.hasValidUser():
      return users.is_current_user_admin()
    else:
      return False

  def getLogOffURL(self):
    return users.create_logout_url(self.request.uri)
```

All the event handlers in the BookmarksBin application are subclasses of
AppHandler (see Chapter 4). Each specialization of this class can validate
if the current user is an administrator and provide customized
administrative behavior, like in Listing 5-5.

Listing 5-5. Customizing Behavior for Admin Users

```
# From bookmarksbin.py
class BookmarksBin(AppHandler):
    .
  def _displayBookmarksPage(self):
    x = {
        'bookmarks': bookmarks,
        'logOffURL': self.getLogOffURL(),
        'bIsAdmin' : self.hasAdminUser() }
    self.renderPage('bookmarksbin.html', x)
```

The customized behavior is carried to the Django template that generates
this page. Listing 5-6 demonstrates how to generate HTML page elements
that are specific to administrative users.

Listing 5-6. HTML Generation for Admin Users

```
<!-- From bookmarksbin.html -->
.
   <h2>
     My Bookmarks
     {% if bIsAdmin %}
     - App Administrator
     {% endif %}
   </h2>
```

Figure 5-7 shows the main application's page output when an admin user is logged on. The additional text won't be generated if the current user isn't an application administrator.

Figure 5-7. User administration customized output

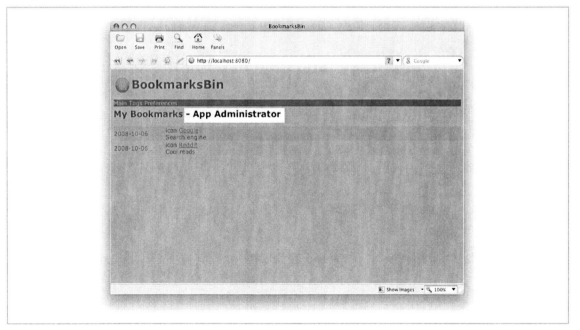

Summary

User handling is done through interaction with the Users and Datastore APIs, depending on the degree of desired functionality. Because programmers don't have control over cookies or session data directly, they rely on these APIs for managing application state and flow. This chapter described the symbiosis between Google Accounts and App Engine applications, how to authenticate users, how to manage preferences and other user-specific behavior, and how set up and customize application flow for admin users.

The next step consists of providing user- and session-specific application behavior. This requires data persistence and granular control over those data. Chapter 6 will describe how to implement these features in the code.

Chapter 6: Using the Datastore

The Datastore is the main scalability feature for Google App Engine applications. Applications written for App Engine are a set of stateless callbacks. This structure allows for distributing requests across an unlimited number of servers. Scalability would be compromised, however, if the application relied on relational database technology for scaling, since requests from multiple servers would somehow have to be tied to some shared connection pool and some kind of shared caching. That would limit applications to using only a subset of Google's servers. It would also invalidate the scalability reasons for putting applications on the cloud and wouldn't be much different from running on a traditional environment.

The Datastore is not a relational database or a facade for one; it is a public API for accessing Google's Bigtable high-performance distributed database system. Bigtable is the reason Google applications and services scale so well and offer users ultrafast response times, much faster than the fastest relational database queries and updates. Therefore, understanding Bigtable concept and how it's architected is helpful before coding data manipulation services for the Datastore.

Bigtable and the Datastore

Bigtable is a Google proprietary technology implemented as a sparse array distributed across multiple servers. Unlike relational databases, it allows for an infinite number of columns and rows. Applications can define new columns on the fly, and the database can scale by simply adding more servers to a cluster. Discrete applications like YouTube and Google Maps each have their own cluster running Bigtable. Figure 6-1 shows the Bigtable architecture and how it relates to application development services.

Figure 6-1. Bigtable architecture

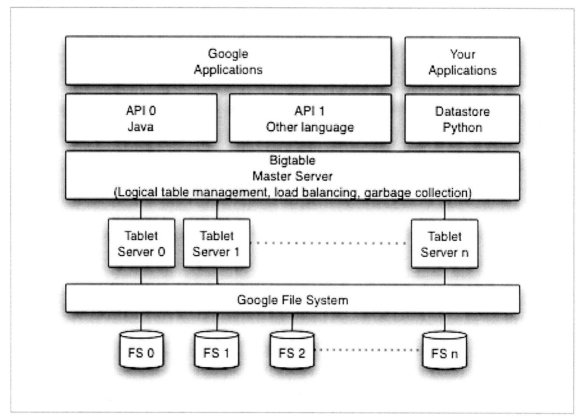

Bigtable consists of a master server that coordinates segments of the larger logical table, called *tablets*, split across a row that makes each tablet of an optimal size (roughly 200MB). Tablets are compressed for optimization purposes and the client API aggressively caches locations and data in either the Google File System (GFS) or in Bigtable itself to eliminate bottlenecks when accessing the data or their metadata, also stored in tablets.

Tip   "Bigtable: A Distributed Storage System for Structured Data," the original paper describing its implementation, is available at http://labs.google.com/papers/bigtable.html.

Bigtable's organization and physical layout diverge from traditional RDBMSs because of their intent: they are optimized for horizontal scalability and performance, trading off the normalization features found in relational databases.

Datastore is the first public API for Bigtable, though the company may release others as its service offerings and Google App Engine evolve. The Official Google Blog and other company publications have described some of the applications that use Bigtable and that at least one other API exists for it already.

The Datastore API

Database operations are defined around entities, or data models. An *entity* is a special kind of object that has one or more properties. Each property is of a specific type (string, user, Boolean, etc.) and can even be recursive or self-referential.

Note   The entity relationship (ER) diagrams from Chapter 3 describe a conceptual view of the BookmarksBin application data model. Though the relationships exist, they won't be implemented like they would in a relational database.

Entities and Unique Identifiers

Entities can be related in one-to-many or many-to-many relationships. Every entity is of a particular kind, either Model or Expando (explained later in this section), and has a unique identifier. Every application entity is of a specific kind; a *kind* is a group of entities returned by a query. Entities in a kind need not have the same properties (i.e., columns in a relational database). The data management concepts are the same as in other data modeling systems, though the terminology can be confusing.

The Datastore assigns `numerid` IDs to unique identifiers unless the application specifies a unique key using the `key_name` argument in its constructor, like in Listing 6-2, which uses the `Owner` entity defined in Listing 6-1. The `Owner` kind is based on the data models described in Figure 3-1 (see Chapter 3).

Table 6-1 clarifies object oriented, relational database, and Datastore terms.

Table 6-1. Datastore, Object-Oriented, and Relational Database Terms

OBJECT ORIENTED	RELATIONAL DATABASE	DATASTORE
Class	Table	Kind
Object	Record	Entity
Attribute	Column	Property

Listing 6-1. owner.py

```
from google.appengine.ext import db

class Owner(db.Model):
    user     = db.UserProperty()
    email    = db.StringProperty()
    nickname = db.StringProperty()
    bOpenNew = db.BooleanProperty()
```

Although the data model describes a unique ID field, this one isn't declared because the `Model` superclass defines and sets it when the entity is saved to the Datastore by executing the `put()` method, as shown in Listing 6-2.

Listing 6-2. Setting Unique Identifiers for Datastore Entities

```
from owner import Owner

def display(anOwner):
    print "owner = "+anOwner.nickname
    if (anOwner.is_saved()):
```

```
        print "key = ", anOwner.key().id_or_name()
    print ""

o0 = Owner(
    email     = "user@domain.com",
    nickname = "pr3d4t0r",
    bOpenNew = False)

o1 = Owner(
    email     = "user2@domain.com",
    nickname = "NikkiWade",
    bOpenNew = False,
    key_name = "NikkiWade")

print 'Content-Type: text/plain'
print ''

o0.put()
o1.put()

display(o0)
display(o1)
```

The unique identifier is generated only after the entity is saved. The runtime will throw an exception if the program tries to invoke its value without saving it first and the exception raise NotSavedError() will appear in the log. The output from Listing 6-2 shows the entities and their associated IDs. In this example, the owner pr3d4t0r got the tenth automatically generated unique identifier, while owner NikkiWade is being managed directly by the application:

```
owner = pr3d4t0r
key =   10
□
owner = NikkiWade
key =   NikkiWade
```

Tip   Explicit, in-program management of `key_name` unique identifiers can become very cumbersome and error prone, so let the Datastore assign those on behalf of the program if possible.

Disallowed Property Names

`key_name` is one of several property names predefined in the model kind. These predefined property names are restricted for use by the Datastore, and applications aren't allowed to use them. Property name rules and restrictions include the following:

- The API ignores any property names beginning with a single underscore (_) in specializations of the `Model` or `Expando` classes. This rule is very useful for storing transient data that don't need to be persisted. Transient variables are those that, by design, should not be saved when an entity is persisted.

- Model class disallowed properties and attributes names like `key` or `key_name` cannot be used in the Python API or in application classes because their semantics are tied to the Datastore.

- The Datastore API reserves all names beginning and ending with double-underscores (_*_); applications must not use them under any circumstances.

The complete list of disallowed property names in `Model` and `Expando` subclasses appears in the Google App Engine documentation. Some users indicated that the list is incomplete and is missing a few disallowed properties. List the properties directly form the `Model` entities by executing this simple Python code: `print dir(myObject)`. Or use the `type()` and `mro` attributes to programmatically get an exhaustive list.

Entity Groups and Transactions

Entity groups comprise all the entities defined at the same level within a hierarchy that can be manipulated in a single transaction. App Engine stores all entities in a group in the same part of the distributed network.

Entities have a hierarchical relationship within a group. An entity can be defined as the *parent* of another, making them both part of the same group. The top entity in this hierarchy, the one without a parent, is a *root entity*; these relationships are established when an entity is created and can't be changed later. All entities that share a common root ancestor are said to be in the same *entity group*.

Tip   An explicit root ancestor isn't always necessary when creating an entity group. Assign a key to the ancestor and define it as the parent of the new entity. This root can be used for defining groups but doesn't need to represent an actual entity itself.

The `Model` constructor defines an initialization parameter, a parent, that may be used for establishing an entity's ancestry. An application may set the parent parameter only at instantiation time, like in Listing 6-6.

Implementing Persistence for the BookmarksBin Application

BookmarksBin persists its data based on user ownership. Figure 6-2 shows the revised entity relationship diagram for this implementation. It highlights the owner entity as the parent in the entity group.

Figure 6-2. Entity relationship and Datastore diagram for BookmarksBin

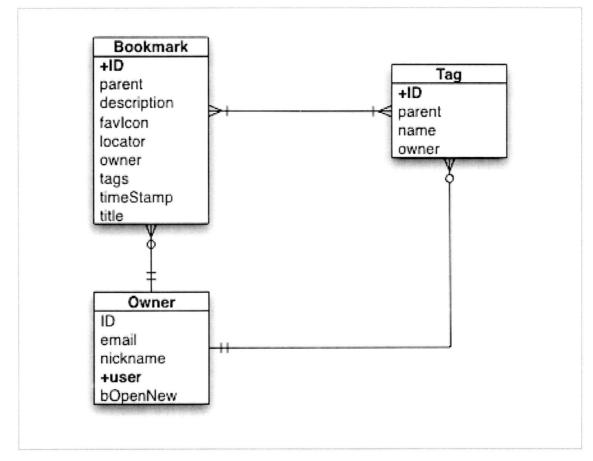

Persisting and Querying an Entity

A user owns one or more bookmarks and has local properties like open_new that define whether a bookmark will open in a new browser or tab or overlay the current BookmarksBin page.

Figure 6-3 shows the execution flow of the application. If the user doesn't have preferences set for an account, the system will not let that user continue to the main page until those preferences are set and persisted.

Figure 6-3. Owner preferences flow

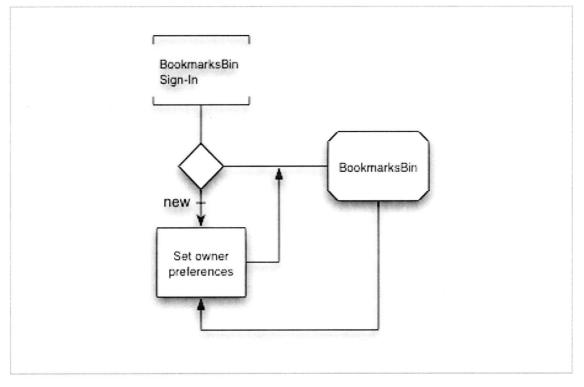

A special handler, UserPreferences, displays the corresponding HTML (defined in the userpreferences.html template), validates whether the user exists in the Datastore using the utility methods from the AppHandler class, and persists the Owner instance if the user chooses to update it. Listing 6-2 shows that the main application will not proceed until the owner preferences are set.

Listing 6-2. Redirecting to a Compulsory Page-Based Current Application State

```
# From the BookmarksBin class event handler:
  def get(self):
    if self.hasValidUser():
      if self.isNewUser():
        self.redirect("/userpreferences")
      else:
        self._displayBookmarksPage()
```

Listing 6-3 has the isNewUser() implementation is implemented in the AppHandler class, the common ancestor for all the event handlers in BookmarksBin.

Listing 6-3. isNewUser() Utility Method Showing Datastore Access

```
# From the AppHandler class:
  def isNewUser(self):
    query = Owner.gql("WHERE user = :1",
        users.get_current_user())
    return (query.count() == 0)
```

The Owner class is a specialization of the db.Model class presented earlier in this chapter. It inherits the gql() class method from db.Model, which provides shorthand for the Google Query Language (GQL) statement SELECT * FROM model and allows the user to define the conditional portion of the statement. Owner entities are keyed on the Google Accounts unique user property associated with users.get_current_user(). Since only one user matches the currently logged on and valid user, the call to `query.count()` will return 1. If it's 0, the user is new to the BookmarksBin application and must define runtime preferences before gaining access to the rest of the application (see Figure 6-3).

The `UserPreferences` class is another specialization of `AppHandler`. This event handler is responsible for displaying the user preferences page and providing the business logic for registering a new user with the application and creating its entity in the Datastore.

The code in Listing 6-4 illustrates how to persist the application preferences for an owner.

Listing 6-4. Handling an Update and Persisting Owner Preferences

```
# From the UserPreferences class:
  def _updateOwnerPreferences(self):
    if (self.request.get('bNewUser') == "True"):
      owner = Owner(
        bOpenNew = self.request.get('bOpenNew')=="True",
        user = users.get_current_user(),
        email = cgi.escape(self.request.get('email')),
        nickname = cgi.escape(
            self.request.get('nickname')))
    else:
      query = Owner.gql("WHERE user = :1",
          users.get_current_user())

      owner = query.get()

      owner.email = cgi.escape(
          self.request.get('email'))
      owner.bOpenNew = self.request.get(
          'bOpenNew'
          ) == "True"
      owner.nickname = cgi.escape(
          self.request.get('nickname'))

    owner.put()
```

```
# *** Public methods ***
def post(self):
    if self.hasValidUser():
        self._updateOwnerPreferences()
        self._displayUserPreferencesPage()
```

Entities are persisted only if the put() method is called on them. The _updateOwnerPreferences() method checks if the current user is new to the application. In that case, the method instantiates a new Owner entity and sets its values. If the owner already existed, the method fetches its instance from the Datastore and updates its values. The owner entity is persisted in the put() call regardless of which execution path was followed.

The first panel in Figure 6-4 shows the default preferences when the owner is new to the system. Notice, for example, that Nickname and Email are the same, the default value for User object as it exists in Google Accounts. The user may update any of these fields, submit the form to the UserPreferences handler, and redisplay the page with the modifications. The user is free to navigate to other parts of the application (bookmarks display, tags management) as soon as the Owner entity exists in the Datastore, because the isNewUser() method will return False from then onward.

Figure 6-4. Default preferences modifications

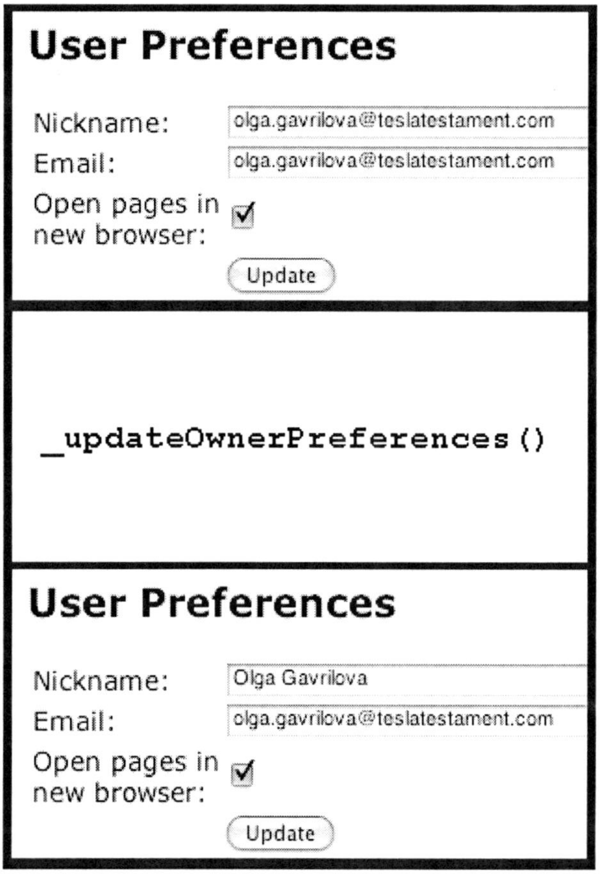

ADDING PAGES AND EVENT HANDLERS TO AN APPLICATION

Figure 6-3 shows that user preferences functionality is handled separately from the main BookmarksBin page and handler. Although you can define every handler in a single class, the resulting code would be hard to read and maintain, because it would contain several logic branches for each event and page rendering.

BookmarksBin defines a separate event handler and associated pages for each component instead. This new functionality is easy to implement by registering a new handler with the WSGIApplication object in the main application class (BookmarksBin in this case).

```
def main():
    application = webapp.WSGIApplication([
        ('/', BookmarksBin),
        ('/userpreferences', UserPreferences)],
        debug=True)
    run_wsgi_app(application)
```

Any inbound request for the /userpreferences pages will be redirected to the UserPreferences handler for processing.

Additional event handlers will be added to the application the same way. This is easier than updating the app.yaml configuration file with new event handlers if the additional functionality is part of the same application, because adding new application handlers to app.yaml requires maintaining an additional set of files. app.yaml also requires defining the new handler's url: in the correct order to avoid having it trapped by the catch-all url: .* or equivalent directive. Defining a custom handler is just more work for no reason if the application event handlers are all related. Use the main application as a dispatcher.

Deciding Which Calls to the Datastore Are Necessary

It's always necessary to query the Datastore for application entities once their data persists in order to track state for these reasons:

- There is no guarantee that the user will connect to the exact same server between calls. The new user may connect to one server for defining preferences and submit the modifications to another server. The Datastore is only consistent method ensure that the entities worked on are in a known state.

- App Engine applications are just a collection of stateless event handlers. Since they don't keep state, every invocation is handled by a potential new instance every time. Member properties only exist for the duration of an event.

Cookies are a good alternative way to minimize the number of queries that an application makes to the Datastore and maintain session if the data are unlikely to change as the user navigates the application.

The bookmarks and tags entity persistence mechanism uses similar techniques as those described in this section.

Associating and Manipulating Entities

Application-level manipulation is straightforward. There is no need for an ORM or any other entity-to-Datastore mapper beyond the DAO-like structure of db.Model and db.Expando. Except for a concession for querying the Datastore implemented in GQL, application programmers can manipulate entities and their attributes using Python-level calls.

Tip The Datastore API provides classes for handling entities, queries, properties, keys, transactions, and so on. Although the library isn't very large, it would take too much space to reproduce in this book. Please keep a copy of the reference in your web browser while following the examples from this chapter `http://code.google.com/appengine/docs/Datastore`.

One-to-Many Relationships

BookmarksBin associates all tags to a specific instance of Owner (see Figure 6-2). A programmer experienced in relational database handling would consider writing a query of some sort for this. App Engine developers most often use the Datastore API and manipulate entities as Python objects, and only resort to explicit queries when fine-tuning the application.

Figure 6-5 is a screenshot of some of the names that a user would tag bookmarks with. An event handler processes add, display, and delete tag requests. Each of these methods could be implemented explicitly by using the Query and GQL facilities or by using each entity's methods for Datastore operations.

Each Tag entity is associated with a specific Owner. A ReferenceProperty is the simplest way to create this association. Listing 6-5 shows how it's created.

Listing 6-5. Tag Class Definition

```
class Tag(db.Model):
    name = db.StringProperty()
    owner = db.ReferenceProperty(Owner,
        collection_name = 'tags')
```

The `owner` property definition states that every `Tag` entity belongs to a specific `Owner`. All `Tag` entities in this association become available to the application as collection property and can be manipulated as standard Python objects, as shown in the next section.

Figure 6-5. Tag management in BookmarksBin

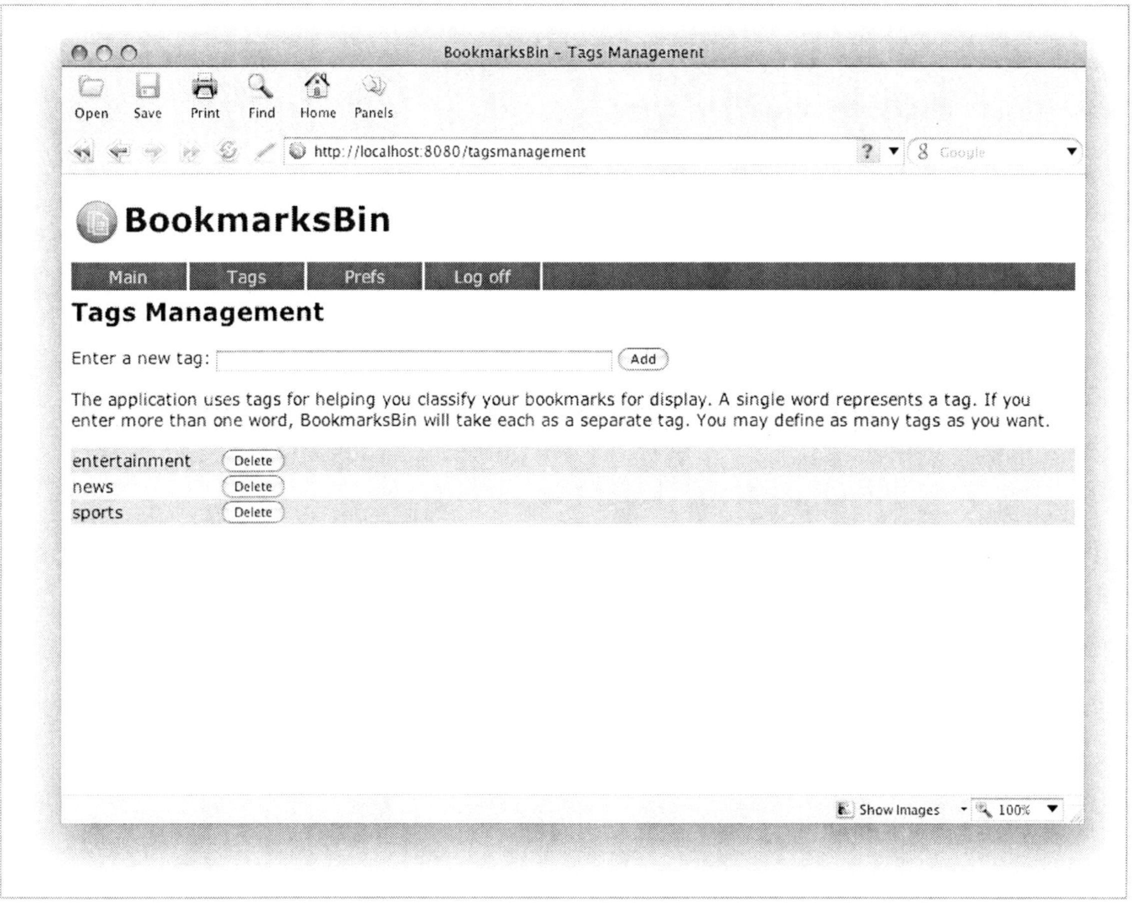

Querying and Adding Entities

How does a programmer manipulate these entities? The methods in Listing 6-6 show how to display and add tags in response to end-user events.

Listing 6-6. Querying and Adding Entities

```
# From tagsmanagement.py

def _fetchAllTags(self):
    return Owner.getCurrent().tags.order('name')

def _addNewTag(self, tagName):
    currentOwner = Owner.getCurrent()
    tags         = currentOwner.tags
    if tagName not in tags:
        tag = Tag(parent = currentOwner,
              name = tagName, owner = currentOwner)
        tag.put()
```

Notice that the tags collection becomes available in the instances of `Owner`. It may be manipulated like any other property, and it establishes the one-to-many relationship between entities of the `Owner` and `Tag` kinds. The `tags` property associated with the `currentOwner` in Listing 6-6 is treated like an in-memory collection. The Datastore infrastructure handles all the entity relationships and associations under the covers.

The `Owner.getCurrent()` class method is a simple utility for fetching the currently logged on user's name and preferences in a single operation defined in Listing 6-7.

Listing 6-7. Owner.getCurrent() Using a Query

```
# From owner.py

@classmethod
def getCurrent(self):
    query = Owner.gql("WHERE user = :1",
          users.get_current_user())
    owner = query.get()
    return owner
```

Now, compare Listing 6-7 against the entities-only implementation of the same method in Listing 6-8.

Listing 6-8. Owner.getCurrent() Using Only Entity Method Calls

```
# From owner.py

    @classmethod
    def getCurrent(self):
        owner = Owner.all().filter('user = ',
            users.get_current_user()).get()
        return owner
```

Entity method calls are a less verbose way of querying the Datastore and will likely feel more natural to a Python programmer. The functionality in both calls is equivalent; the decision which one to use is up to the implementer and the task at hand, as explained in the "Choosing Between Query or GqlQuery?" section later in this chapter.

Deleting an Entity Using db.Query

The method in Listing 6-9 shows the explicit mechanism for deleting an entity from the Datastore.

Listing 6-9. Deleting an Entity

```
# From tagsmanagement.py
    def _deleteTag(self):
        tagName = self.request.get('tag')
        query = db.Query(Tag)
        query.filter(
            "owner = ", Owner.getCurrent()).filter(
            "name = ", tagName)

        results = query.fetch(1)
        if (len(results) > 0):
            results[0].delete()
```

Tag names are unique for each owner's account. The query in Listing 6-9 finds the first matching tag, and the delete() method call removes it from both the collection in the owner's reference property and from the Datastore itself.

Choosing Between Query and GqlQuery

Applications can implement data manipulation through entity method calls, as described earlier in this chapter. The Datastore API provides additional resources for fine-grained data manipulation through the `Query` and `GqlQuery` classes.

The `Query` class provides a Datastore API for preparing queries based on application-defined entities. Listing 6-9 shows a query being created for manipulating `Tag` entities. The API offers Python-level calls and mechanisms for filtering results based on those entities' properties. All data manipulation activities occur by manipulating the query and entities themselves.

`GqlQuery` is the lowest-level querying API for the Datastore. It uses the App Engine GQL language, and it's limited to data searches and retrieval operations (`get()`, `fetch()`, `count()`, etc.).

The main difference between the two lies in how results are accessed and retrieved in response to a query. If `GqlQuery` uses a GQL statement containing `LIMIT` or `OFFSET` clauses, all results are fetched from the call to the Datastore, and iterating through the results happens entirely in memory. In contrast, iteration over `Query` results takes place in small batches and multiple Datastore reads.

Figure 6-6. Iterating Over GqlQuery or Query Result Sets

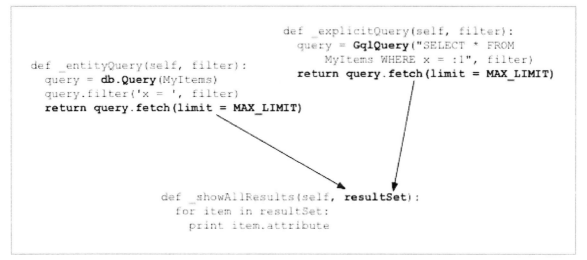

```
                                    def _explicitQuery(self, filter):
                                        query = GqlQuery("SELECT * FROM
                                            MyItems WHERE x = :1", filter)
  def _entityQuery(self, filter):          return query.fetch(limit = MAX_LIMIT)
     query = db.Query(MyItems)
     query.filter('x = ', filter)
     return query.fetch(limit = MAX_LIMIT)




            def _showAllResults(self, resultSet):
                for item in resultSet:
                    print item.attribute
```

Using one or the other is a tuning decision based on each application's characteristics. The query results usage is identical from the programmer's point of view (see Figure 6-6).

The Google Query Language

In the App Engine forums, programmers often ask, "Why is GQL necessary if db.Query and application-level entities can manipulate the Datastore directly?"

The main reason is that GQL implements syntactic sugar to support !=, IN, and other operators that would otherwise require multiple calls to the filter(), fetch(), order(), and other entity methods.

GQL looks like a subset of SQL to the untrained eye. In reality, it lacks most of SQL's verbs and functionality. It's very powerful at executing complex queries against the Datastore, but it implements no other operations like UPDATE, JOIN, or DELETE.

Listing 6-10 is the GQL equivalent to the query from Listing 6-9 for
finding a specific tag in the Datastore.

Listing 6-10. Sample GQL Statement

```
SELECT * FROM Tag WHERE owner = :1 AND name = :2
```

A GQL statement always returns every property for every entity in a result
set; the SELECT prop1, prop2 statement is invalid and will throw an
exception. Since there is no way around always using SELECT * for
queries, the Model and Query classes provide the gql() method that
generates the wildcard SELECT statement, plus the entity kind, as part of the
query, simplifying the programmer's job to providing the conditional test

```
WHERE owner = :1 AND name = :2
```

like in Listings 6-3 and 6-7.

Specifying Conditional Clauses

A conditional clause always specifies a property name and a comparison
operator, such as =, !=, IN, followed by one of the following, depending on
the property's type:

- A Python str literal

- A bound parameter value

- A scalar type like float or integer

- A Boolean literal

Bound parameters can be keywords or positional arguments passed to the
entity's gql() method or the GqlQuery constructor. Listing 6-10 uses
positional arguments, and it's up to the programmer to pass the appropriate

ones when defining the query, like in the first example from Listing 6-11. For keyword-bound parameters, the keyword corresponds to a context-specific parameter that will be substituted when the query executes.

Listing 6-11. Queries and Bound Parameters

```
# Positional:
query = Tag.gql(
    "WHERE owner = :1 AND name = :2",
    Owner.getCurrent(), aString)

# Keyword:
query = Tag.gql(
    "WHERE owner = :owner AND name = :name",
    Owner.getCurrent(), aString)
```

Indexing Entities in the Datastore

App Engine provides automatic index generation based on the queries that it executes. The indexes are defined in a special configuration file, index.yaml, which is automatically updated every time that the development server runs a query for which an index hasn't been defined. It's possible to rely on this automatic index generation for the most part, though developers may tune the indexes manually if desired.

Tip   App Engine will not execute a query for which it's missing an index. Ensure that index.yaml has valid index definitions for every application query.

The Datastore fetches results directly from the index corresponding to a query. It does this by keeping an index for every potential query that an application intends to make, and it updates the indexes with the correct results as the application updates the entities it contains.

Automatic Indexing and Queries

The application has an index for each kind, entity, filter, operator, and sorting order used in a query. Listing 6-12 shows the GQL query that will return every tag associated with an application user, sorted in descending order by name.

Caution   Saying "every tag" is a bit of a stretch. App Engine restricts `fetch()` to retrieving only 1,000 results, regardless of the actual size of the result set, to lower resource utilization. `fetch()` also supports specifying the starting offset, so queries that return more than 1,000 results could be implemented in repeated calls to `fetch()`, using an iterator and an offset multiplier for each iteration, for example, `fetch(1000, nIteration*1000)` where `nIteration` is in `range(0, SOME_LIMIT)`.

Listing 6-12. A Sample Application Query

```
# From modelsdisplay.py
def queryExample():
  query = db.GqlQuery(
      "SELECT * FROM Tag WHERE owner = :1 \
      ORDER BY name DESC",
      Owner.getCurrent())
  results = query.fetch(1000)
  return results
```

The development application server creates a configuration entry like in Listing 6-13 and updates `index.yaml` with the query kinds, sorting order, and so on, as well as the number of times that it was executed.

Listing 6-13. index.yaml Sample Entry

```
# AUTOGENERATED
.
.
# Used 42 times in query history.
```

```
- kind: Tag
  properties:
  - name: owner
  - name: name
    direction: desc
```

The Datastore keeps indexes for each kind, filter property, operator, and sort order used in a query. The application shares the same index among any queries of the same form even if the filter values are different.

Indices are tables of keys for entities/filters/operators/order combinations. The Datastore executes them in this sequence:

- Identify the query's corresponding index based on its structure.

- Scan the index at the first entity that meets all the filtering conditions based on the specific query value.

- Return each entity found and continue scanning until no conditions are met or until reaching the end of the index.

An index table contains columns for all properties used in a filter or sorting operation. The Datastore puts all results of every possible indexed query in consecutive rows of the table and orders them by each row's resulting property values in this manner:

- Ancestors

- Equality or IN filters

- Inequality filters

- Sort order

Defining Indexes Manually

Developers may define application indexes in the index.yaml configuration file if the ones generated by the development application server aren't sufficient. All that's needed is for the developer to define the indexes anywhere above the # AUTOGENERATED comment in the configuration file, like in listing 6-14.

Listing 6-14. Manual Update of index.yaml

```
indexes:
# This index was entered manually by the developer:
- kind: Owner
  properties:
  - name: user


# AUTOGENERATED


# Used once in query history.
- kind: Tag
  properties:
  - name: owner
  - name: name
```

THE DEVELOPMENT APPLICATION SERVER AND INDEX MANAGEMENT

A query will fail if App Engine executes it without a valid configuration in index.yaml. If the application generates every possible query during the development phase, the development application server will generate the indexes as it finds them and update the index.yaml file accordingly. Any missing indexes must be edited and managed manually in index.yaml.

Indexes contain only entities for which the index refers to every one of their properties. An entity won't appear in the index if it lacks an indexed property and thus will never be the result of any query. Finally, not all properties are indexable. Entities of the types BlobProperty or TextProperty are never indexed, so queries based on them are impossible.

Indexes That Are Not Created by App Engine

Indexes are *not* built directly as a result of updating the application to `appspot.com`! App Engine creates or updates the indexes in a different, lower priority process separate from the upload. If both `index.yaml` and the application are uploaded at the same time, the application may throw errors when running queries until the indexes are updated.

Tip   According to Google, it's best to update the `index.yaml` file several hours before uploading the application to `appspot.com` to allow plenty of time for building the indexes before the new application version uses them. Use this command for the updates: `appcfg.py upload_indices yourappdir`.

Restrictions on Queries

The Datastore imposes these restrictions on queries executed by App Engine applications:

- You can't query, sort, or filter an entity that's missing a specific property; remember that entities of the same kind are not required to all have the same properties.

- Inequality filters are only allowed in one property per query across all its filters.

- Sorting on inequality filters must occur before other sort orders.

Tip   A complete list of workarounds for these restrictions is available at `http://code.google.com/appengine/docs/Datastore/queriesandindexes.html`.

Committing Data in Transactions

A *transaction* is a group of Datastore operations that either succeed or fail. If all of the operations in the set succeed, then all of their effects apply to the Datastore. Entity groups are required for implementing transactions, since all grouped entities are stored in the same Datastore node. Multiple entities can be modified or added in a single transaction as long as all of them have a parent that's part of a given entity group.

An ancestor entity can be deleted at any time without affecting its descendants. A program may access any of the descendants by using its complete Key or path.

Transactions can only perform operations on entity groups that share a common root entity and don't allow ad hoc queries; transactional retrievals are accomplished using keys and the `db.get()` function, both explained earlier in this chapter. An entity can be created or modified only once per transaction, and transactions may be invoked more than once if they fail during the first call. Transactions may fail if a different user or process attempts to update entities in the same group at the same time. The Datastore will automatically attempt the operation multiple times and raise a `TransactionFailedException` if it fails. The user may retry or roll back the transaction.

Reasons for Using Transactions

An application's critical operation may fail and make it necessary to retry or at least notify the user. Some common causes of failure include:

- Internal application errors or incomplete data

- High contention rate due to too many users interacting with the same resource in a busy server

- Resource quota limits come into effect

- External resource service request fails

Any of these problems may occur in the middle of an operation, so you need to provide a mechanism that ensures that all grouped operations either succeed or fail together, to ensure data consistency and referential integrity for the application. Datastore operations like `put()` and `delete()` are atomic (i.e., they either fail or succeed 100 percent), but failure may occur during method execution in between `put()` or `delete()` operations for more than one entity.

Using the Transaction API

App Engine transactions can execute one or more Python and Datastore operations as a group and their effects may be permanent unless one of them raises an exception. The operations are defined in a Python function accessible by the calling object and executed using the library function `db.run_in_transaction()`, using the application's function as an argument. Any set of operations that must complete or fail together are excellent candidates for a transaction. Listing 6-15 is an example of the general coding pattern for executing a transaction in App Engine.

Listing 6-15. Executing a Transaction and Handling Exceptions

```
while nRetries < 3 and not bSuccessful:
  try:
    db.run_in_transaction(commitBookmark,
        aBookmark, tagsList, entityParent)
    bSuccessful = True
  except db.TransactionFailedError:
    nRetries++
  finally:
    if not bSuccessful:
      errorMessage = "Unable to save bookmark"
```

This naïve example assumes that the only problem with a commit would be the Datastore's availability and that recovery may be possible after a fixed number of retries.

Tip   A complete list of all the Datastore exceptions is available at http://code.google.com/appengine/docs/Datastore/exceptions.html.

The `db.run_in_transaction()` function accepts the `commitBookmark()` Python function as its first argument, followed by a bookmark to add, all the tags associated with that bookmark, and the parent entity so that all these items are stored in the same entity group. Committing these changes in a transaction makes sense, because bookmarks and tags have a many-to-many relationship, and updates must occur with more than one entity for the operation to complete successfully.

Many-to-Many Relationships

You'll implement many-to-many entity associations in the Datastore API differently than you do in relational databases (RDBs).

RDBs are optimized for performance and compactness, and data normalization is a good practice that leads do minimizing the storage requirements for the database.

Datastore is designed for scalability on commodity server farms; App Engine developers should not worry about the cost of storage space and focus on scaling the application. This focus leads to the implementation of many-to-many relationships in the database as tablets of associations between items of one kind with those of another. Remember, too, that entities in the same group are stored in the same Datastore node. As an example, many-to-many relationships between bookmarks and tags can be represented by the example in Table 6-2.

Table 6-2. Many-to-Many Example

BOOKMARK	TAG
TheServerSide	News
TheServerSide	Java
TheServerSide	Development
CNN	News
Reddit	News

Table 6-2. Many-to-Many Example (Continued)

BOOKMARK	TAG
Reddit	Entertainment
Reddit	Development

The example in Table 6-2 doesn't use storage space very efficiently and isn't elegant or normalized, but it's easy to implement and scale. Datastore and entity manipulation are optimized for a specific user's data, since all the entities will persist in the same node by being in the same entity group as depicted in Figure 6-7, and new nodes may be added quickly to fulfill storage and entity manipulation demand.

Figure 6-7. The BookmarksBin entity group

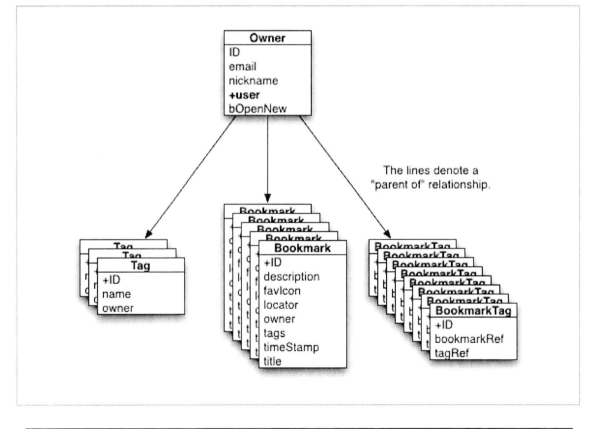

Access to entities is fast, because all the elements of the entity group have immediate access to other members, through their ancestor relationships (BookmarkTag entities that have the same Owner as a parent), through explicit relationships between entity instances (Tag or Bookmark entities have same entity as Owner and parent), or through both. Having an instance of the owner architected into the application as a side-effect of signing in to the application's account or having the unique entity key or path provides immediate access to any entity that depends on it and to its properties. There is no need for an explicit JOIN: the entity group already joins all the entities.

Storing and Deleting Entities

Figure 6-8 shows how a user interacts with the main bookmark management screen. Users may add or delete bookmarks and assign one or more tags to the bookmarks by selecting them from an options box.

Adding or deleting a bookmark entity involves manipulation of the Bookmark and Tag entities and updates to the BookmarkTag reference to associate them. Adding bookmarks and deleting either bookmarks or tags affects both sets so these operations are good candidates for implementing them in transactions.

Listing 6-16. Adding Bookmarks in a Transaction

```
# From bookmarksbin.py
def commitBookmark(aBookmark, tagsList, theParent):
  aBookmark.put()
  for tag in tagsList:
    BookmarkTag(
        bookmark = aBookmark, tag = tag,
        parent = theParent).put()
  .
class BookmarksBin(AppHandler):
    .
  def _addBookmark(self):
```

```python
tagNames = self.request.get_all('tags')
bookmark = Bookmark(
    parent = Owner.getCurrent(),
    description = cgi.escape(
        self.request.get('description')),
    favIcon = None, # implemented later
    locator = cgi.escape(
        self.request.get('locator')),
    title = None, # implemented later
    owner = Owner.getCurrent())

tagsList = list()
if len(tagNames) < 1:
    tagsList.append(None)
else:
    for tagName in tagNames:
        tagsList.append(Tag.getTagFor(tagName))

db.run_in_transaction(
    commitBookmark, bookmark,
    tagsList, Owner.getCurrent())
```

Figure 6-8. The BookmarksBin main page

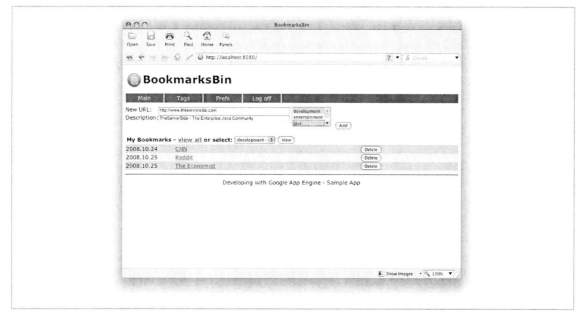

Storing Entities in a Transaction

Listing 6-16 shows the implementation of the add event handler. The _addBookmark() method initializes the tags list and the new Bookmark instance. These initializations take place outside of the transactional function, because getting the references to all the applicable tags requires the getTagFor(aTagName) query, and queries aren't allowed in the middle of a transaction. The transaction defined in commitBookmark() persists the Bookmark and its related tags.

The original definition for BookmarkTag stored the Bookmark and Tag entities unique IDs, a habit from implementing similar operations in relational databases. The object-oriented database (OODB) nature of Datastore, and the availability of ReferenceProperty properties obviate this approach. Each instance of BookmarkTag allows direct access to both the bookmark and a specific tag without having to execute additional queries, a very powerful feature of Datastore entities.

Deleting Entities in a Transaction

Removing a bookmark or a tag from the application's Datastore requires updates to the set of `BookmarkTag` entities that relate all the entities involved. The code in listing 6-17 shows how to delete a bookmark and all references to a tag, and vice versa.

Listing 6-17. Deleting a Bookmark or a Tag and All Its Relations

```
# From bookmarksbin.py
def deleteBookmarkAndAssociations(
    aBookmark, references):
  for reference in references:
    reference.delete()
  aBookmark.delete()

.
class BookmarksBin(AppHandler):
    .
  def _deleteBookmark(self):
    nID = int(self.request.get('bookmarkID'))
    bookmark = Bookmark.get_by_id(
        nID, Owner.getCurrent())
    references = BookmarkTag.all().filter(
        'bookmark = ', bookmark).fetch(1000)
    db.run_in_transaction(
        deleteBookmarkAndAssociations,
        bookmark, references)
    return None

# From tagsmanagement.py
def deleteTagAndAssociations(tag, relationships):
  for relatedBookmark in relationships:
    relatedBookmark.delete()
  tag.delete()
```

Finding the appropriate bookmark is very simple. The bookmarks list on the HTML page includes the entity's ID in a hidden input. Clicking Delete dispatches this to the `BookmarksBin` event handler. Notice that the `get_by_id()` function must specify the ID and the parent and failing to do so will return `None`. This is necessary for grouped entities.

The transactional functions for deleting associations in both listings have identical implementations and just happen to operate on entities of different kinds. Since the `delete()` method is defined in `db.Model`, the function could be written as a general purpose one-to-many delete method.

WHAT'S WITH THE 1,000 MAGIC NUMBER?

Every query in these examples with "get all" semantics has a 1,000 magic number cap. That's because the App Engine preview release caps queries to return that maximum number. If the query is likely to return more than 1,000 items you may specify offsets to the `fetch()` method that describe where to start fetching entities. Please refer to the App Engine online API documentation for more details.

Summary

The Datastore provides an efficient, scalable persistence mechanism for App Engine applications. It offers the programmer features for storing, querying, and deleting data in the form of entities and allows transactional commits for operations involving entities from the same group. The Datastore exposes a public API for the Google Bigtable mechanism, a nonrelational database system designed for storing and searching massive amounts of data across multiple commodity servers. Designing the data access objects (and their related operations) for an application using Datastore is more akin to designing for an object database, because a traditional relational model isn't implemented.

BookmarksBin executes queries against Datastore in every page that it displays, which may result in extraneous stressing of the App Engine that may stop the application from working, since application resources are capped, and too many Datastore accesses may result in reaching that cap faster than the application should. Some of these data could be stored in cookies instead, or they could be stored in Memcache, a high-performance key-value cache described in the next chapter.

Chapter 7: Memcache and Session Data

The stateless nature of a Google App Engine application necessitates end-user data persistence in some mechanism that will survive multiple calls across multiple servers, since there is no guarantee that two sequential calls to an event handler will execute in the same server. This stateless nature precludes the use of traditional session data mechanisms, since sessions tend to be tied to a specific server. Scalable architectures that use multiple servers for session handling also implement some mechanism for caching and sharing session-specific data. Google App Engine is not an exception.

Chapter 6 described how to persist the application state using the Datastore. Although effective and easy to use, Datastore operations tax system resources and I/O. The more application users and the more data they work on, the higher the resource consumption. Data could also persist in cookies, albeit with the limitations imposed by the browser environment. Neither solution is enough, by itself, to provide a good way of persisting application state for short-term, mostly read-only purposes. Google App Engine introduced Memcache for this purpose.

What Is Memcache?

Memcache is a service that provides a key-value caching mechanism for efficient in-memory data retrieval across multiple instances of an App Engine application. The Memcache API enables

- A reduction in the number of Datastore queries
- A reduction in the Datastore quota usage for popular pages
- Caching of expensive query results
- Implementation of transient counters

Data in Memcache are available to every instance of an application and only discarded due to cache exhaustion. Although the policies for data exhaustion aren't explicit to application developers, available documentation hints that it's quite high.

Well behaved applications that rely on caching tend to set an expiration time for individual items in the cache or for the whole application. The Memcache API provides support for both.

MEMCACHE ORIGINS

memcached is an open-source, distributed object caching API available for every major application programming language. It was developed by Danga Interactive as the data optimization mechanism used by LiveJournal. The memcached implementation is simple and elegant: start a server that manages a large hash table, and call the client API to add items to it. Its usage pattern is very simple too: query the cache, and get whatever it stores using a specific key. That's it! More information about memcached is available at `http://www.danga.com/memcached/`.

Applications access data by a unique key, and the user has the option of setting up the data expiration time. Cache invalidation and refreshment are left to the implementation for the most part, since the developers know best about what needs to be persisted and when it becomes invalid.

Tip   The Memcache API defines both a client- and function-based API. The client is just a wrapper around the function API, with the same exact function names and argument parameters. The complete API is available at `http://code.google.com/appengine/docs/memcache/`.

Figure 7-1 shows the basic implementation pattern for Memcache requests.

Figure 7-1. Making a Memcache request from an application

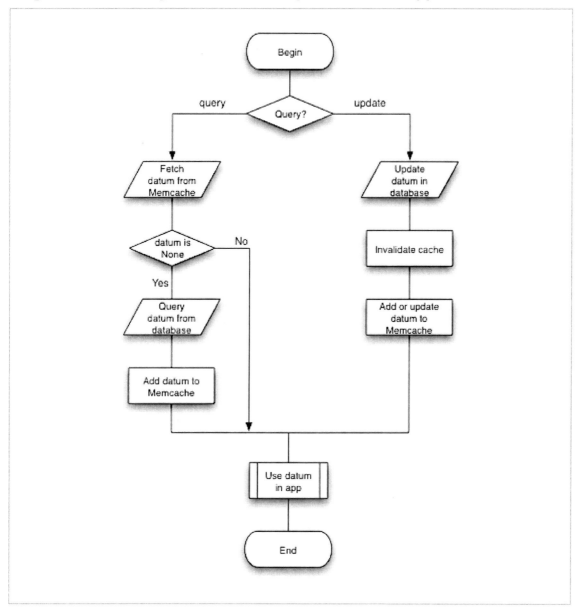

Using Memcache for Session Data

BookmarksBin uses the currently signed in user to create an application owner entity that stores application- and session-specific data. The owner is the root ancestor to all the application entities (the owner itself, the bookmarks, and the tags), as described in the previous chapter. Since all session activity depends on the owner, every usage of any persisted data results in a query. Executing queries on every page interaction is inefficient over the application lifetime, since Owner instances are unique per session, and they would execute a query every time they're used.

Caching the Session Owner

The entity keys are unique across the Memcache calls. Memcache itself doesn't know anything about the session where it runs, so a naïve implementation of Memcache for the session owner may look like the code in Listing 7-1.

Listing 7-1. Owner Entity Naïve Memcache Usage

```
# From owner.py:
  @classmethod
  def getCurrent(self):
    owner = memcache.get("owner")
    if owner is None:
      owner = Owner.all().filter('user = ',
          users.get_current_user()).get()
      memcache.add(
          "owner", owner,
          apptools.DAY_AS_SECONDS)

    return owner
```

Using a generic key like owner will have bad side effects. In this case, the key will live in the cache once it's defined, and every cached request will return the owner's data corresponding to the first user who set the entry in the cache, not the one associated with the current session. Consider this scenario:

- User Bob logs on to BookmarksBin to update his bookmarks and profile. This sets the Owner instance in the cache globally since the owner name is not unique.

- User Alice logs on to BookmarksBin to view her daily news links. They appear to be gone! Instead, she'd get a reference to Bob's Owner instance, including his nickname and preferences.

In some cases, data may be cached across all instances of the application (these cases are easier to implement), and at other times, the data must be session specific. Listing 7-2 shows a better example of session-specific cache keys that will result in individual users getting their own data.

Listing 7-2. Owner Entity Memcache Implementation

```
import apptools
from google.appengine.api import memcache
from google.appengine.api import users
from google.appengine.ext import db

def ownerKey():
  return "User.email="+users.get_current_user().email()

class Owner(db.Model):
  user     = db.UserProperty()
  email    = db.StringProperty()
  nickname = db.StringProperty()
  bOpenNew = db.BooleanProperty()

  def put(self):
    super(Owner, self).put()

    memcache.delete(ownerKey())
    memcache.add(
        ownerKey(), self, apptools.DAY_AS_SECONDS)
```

```
@classmethod
def getCurrent(self):
  owner = memcache.get(ownerKey())

  if owner is None:
    owner = Owner.all().filter('user = ',
        users.get_current_user()).get()
    memcache.add(
        ownerKey(), owner,
        apptools.DAY_AS_SECONDS)

  return owner
```

This implementation defines the key in terms of a relatively unique piece of information, unlikely to be the same for more than one user across the system (see the limitations on user e-mail attributes in Chapter 5). A utility method, ownerKey(), takes the current user from Google Accounts, gets the e-mail address, and defines a cache key that way. The getCurrent() method is now much more efficient, because it needs to fetch only the current Owner instance based on this key or update the cache if it hasn't been initialized.

If the user invalidates any account data, like the nickname or the preference to open bookmarked pages in a new browser, then the Owner instance must perform the appropriate update, invalidate the cache, and update that object as well. The Owner instances thus override the default put() implementation from db.Model to perform these actions.

Implementing Memcache Calls with Entities

Should entities implement Memcache calls? Like most things in applied computer programming, the answer is, "It depends." Using entities made sense in the Owner class to illustrate one implementation style. Since cache invalidation occurs during Datastore updates, and in this case, the only possible update is put(), adding the Memcache calls in here was logical.

Examples later in this chapter perform Memcache operations, because the application execution flow isn't specific to an entity or entity group. In those cases, the cached data is relevant to an event handler, for example, `bookmarksbin.py`. There is no always-correct answer to this question. You'll need to analyze the application usage and implement caching accordingly.

Defining Unique Key Names

Session-specific storage and code reusability are two of the reasons for defining unique key names for Memcache entries. Software expert Roy Leban suggested a naming convention for Google App Engine developers' key names that will aid in addressing these. The suggestions are summarized in table 7-1.

Table 7-1. Suggested Naming Conventions for Memcache References

CASE	FORMAT	UNIQUE VALUE
Model instance	Model.field=unique	Field value
Class instance	ClassName.attribute=unique	Attribute value
Class data	ClassName.meaning:unique	Meaning-specific value

The session-specific keys in this chapter are based on these recommendations and prepend the `Owner` instance's `id_or_name` attribute. That's because tags and bookmarks are also specific to an owner in the context of the application. Any other unique attribute could be applied.

Note   See Roy Leban's Memcache in Reusable Code blog posting for further discussion of the key naming convention: `http://www.thisdev.com/2008/08/memcache-in-reusable-code.html`.

Using Memcache Services Throughout an Application

BookmarksBin tags are good candidates for caching, because the application often queries for individual items among them. The methods in Listing 7-3 showcase the Memcache calls implemented in the `Tag` entity.

Listing 7-3. Memcache Usage in the Tag Entity

```python
# From tag.py:
class Tag(db.Model):
  .

  .
  def delete(self):
    name = self.name
    super(Tag, self).delete()

    memcache.delete(Tag.cacheKeyFor(name))

  def put(self):
    super(Tag, self).put()

    memcache.delete(Tag.cacheKeyFor(self.name))
    memcache.add(
        Tag.cacheKeyFor(self.name), self,
        apptools.DAY_AS_SECONDS)

  @classmethod
  def cacheKeyFor(self, tagName):
    cacheKey  = str(
        Owner.getCurrent().key().id_or_name())
    cacheKey += ".Tag.name="+tagName

    return cacheKey

  @classmethod
  def getTagFor(self, aName):
```

```
cacheKey = Tag.cacheKeyFor(aName)
tag = memcache.get(cacheKey)

if tag is None:
  tag = self.all().filter('owner = ',
    Owner.getCurrent()).filter(
        'name = ', aName).get()
  memcache.add(
      cacheKey, tag, apptools.DAY_AS_SECONDS)

return tag
```

The `Tag` entity participates in its own persistence like all Datastore objects, and it makes sense again to provide caching for the numerous single-tag queries it may receive. Therefore, it overrides the `put()` and `delete()` methods to cache the individual entities as they are updated in the Datastore.

The `cacheKeyFor()` method generates a key in the form `42.Tag.name=news`. It uses the current owner's unique ID to ensure that the generated key applies only to the user logged on to the application. Key collisions could happen if this ID wasn't used and two or more users decided to define a common word like "news" as a tag.

Caching Data from Complex Queries

Most of the caching operations described so far aim to satisfy requests for single data items with simple key-value pair relationships. An application may implement dynamic querying capabilities that cannot be anticipated at coding time. Usage patterns may emerge from such queries that would benefit from caching the results.

The code in Listing 7-4 shows the how BookmarksBin queries for all the bookmarks associated with a specific tag when the user filters the list; the class generates unique keys based on the query type and the current user's unique ID in the form `42.BookmarkTag.for:news`.

Listing 7-4. Caching Complex Queries

```python
# From bookmarksbin.py
class BookmarksBin(AppHandler):
    .
    .
    .
    def _filterBookmarksFor(self, tag):
        cacheKey = self._allBooksForTagKey(tag)
        bookmarks = memcache.get(cacheKey)

        if bookmarks is None:
            if tag == u'unclassified':
                bookmarks = Bookmark.getAll()
            else:
                bookmarks = [x.bookmark
                    for x in BookmarkTag.all().filter(
                        'tag = ',
                        Tag.getTagFor(tag)).fetch(LIMIT)]
                bookmarks.sort(
                    key=operator.attrgetter('description'))

            memcache.add(cacheKey, bookmarks,
                7*apptools.DAY_AS_SECONDS)

        return bookmarks
```

This query consumes more resources because of the variability in the number of bookmarks associated with a given tag. Adding new tags doesn't invalidate these cache entries, because new tags will return empty lists when queried. Adding new bookmarks should invalidate the cache if new entries are associated with existing caching keys. The invalidation policies will evolve from usage patterns and application performance analysis.

Invalidating the Cache

The Memcache API provides several ways of invalidating the cache. Each is used in response to the application developer's requirements regarding the staleness of the cache or the Datastore updates policy. None of these calls is right or wrong; rather, each is used depending on the context for invalidating the cache:

- `delete()`: Used for deleting a specific key from Memcache without disturbing other entries.
- `delete_multi()`: Used for deleting a list of keys from Memcache while leaving others in place. This function also provides an argument for setting a prefix for every key in the cache and is useful for identifying session-specific keys that must be removed from the cache.
- `flush_all()`: The nuclear option. A call to this function wipes out all entries from Memcache across the whole application.

Other Memcache Functions

The Memcache API provides functions for setting, fetching, or adding data to the cache individually or in groups. These functions provide convenient wrappers that implement common implementation patterns for the basic functions already discussed in this chapter. The Google App Engine documentation provides a complete list of these functions and the parameters that they operate on.

Summary

Applications that rely on the Datastore for all their runtime queries consume more resources, are less responsive, and ultimately may have a negative effect on the App Engine usage quotas. Memcache provides an elegant mechanism for enabling sessionwide and applicationwide data available for runtime manipulation in the form of simple key-value pairs in which values represent a single data element, a whole list, a whole page, or any other data that can otherwise persist in the Datastore.

So far, all the chapters in this book have dealt with the implementation underpinnings of a Google App Engine application. The next two chapters will present the features for manipulating images, fetching URLs from third-party servers, and managing the application itself. Let's begin those discussions by updating the BookmarksBin application to work with images in the next chapter.

Chapter 8: Mail, URL Fetching, and Image Manipulation

Google App Engine is an evolving platform. It was released as a preview, and Google added new features as this book was being written and will possibly offer even more by the time you read it.

This chapter presents the App Engine utility APIs, a set of classes, objects, and functions for enhancing an application's capabilities. They include

- The *Mail API* for sending messages from web applications
- The *URL Fetch API* for communicating with other hosts over HTTP and HTTPS
- The *Images API* for server-side image manipulation

All these APIs come built in with App Engine.

Sending E-mail

BookmarksBin users may want to share a bookmark with a friend by e-mail. The bookmarks depicted in Figure 8-1 now include a new button for each link labeled Share. Clicking it opens a window where the user can verify the bookmark and its URL and enter an e-mail address to send the link.

Configuring dev_appserver.py

The development application server offers the ability to send e-mail through a mail transfer agent (MTA) configured from the command line. Execute `dev_appserver.py --help` to view all the configurable options:

- `--smtp_host=HOSTNAME` defines the SMTP host or relay for sending email. A blank value disables SMTP.

- `--smtp_password=PASSWORD` defines the password for the SMTP server defined in `smtp_host`.

- `--smtp_port=PORT` sets the port used for SMTP communication; 25 is the default port for e-mail.

- `--smtp_user=USER` is the user required by the SMTP host for sending e-mail. The development application server will only try to connect and use the password if this argument is not empty.

Tip   Check with the system administrator or ISP to find out which of these parameters are required for sending e-mail from your development workstation.

Figure 8-1. The Share Bookmark window

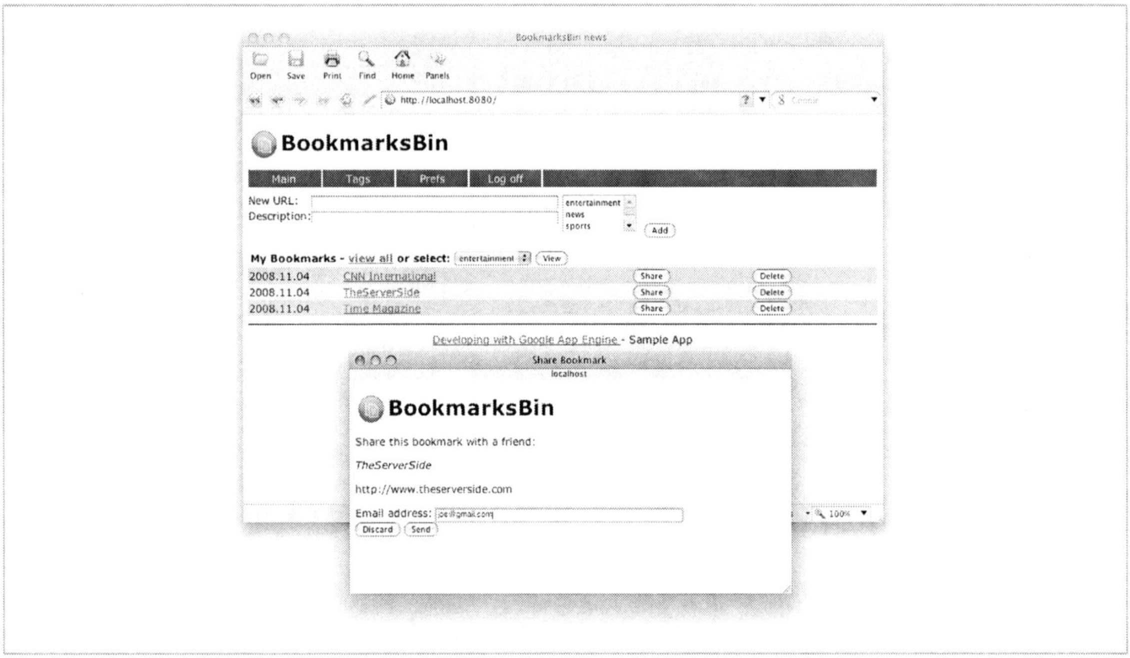

Keep in mind that calls to the Mail API won't send any messages unless the development server starts with at least the `--smtp_host` server parameter.

Configuring the App Engine to Send Mail

Unlike the with the development application server, App Engine doesn't require any end-user configuration for sending e-mail. It relies instead on Gmail and uses the current user's e-mail account. The Mail API requires the sender's e-mail address to be the same as the Google Accounts ID or Gmail account, and the Mail API will throw an exception if no e-mail address is defined or if Google doesn't manage the e-mail address.

Note   Once it becomes generally available, App Engine will support e-mail addresses from domains managed by Google Domains. Until then, limit addresses to use the user's Gmail account or Google Accounts ID.

E-mail sent from the development application server will appear to come from whatever user name was used for logging into the test application.

There are no mail transfer agent configuration parameters that application users or administrators can modify when using the Mail API.

Sending E-mail From an Application

The Share Bookmark window is just an HTML form launched by clicking a bookmark's Share button. There are two basic approaches for handling the event: through a dedicated new handler instance or by updating the functionality in an existing handler. BookmarksBin follows the second approach, since sending a bookmark, it may be argued, is an activity in the application's main area of concern. Listing 8-1 shows the event handler implementation.

Listing 8-1. A Naïve Implementation for Sending E-mail from the Application

```python
# From bookmarksbin.py:

def _dispatchEmailTo(self, email, nID):
    owner = Owner.getCurrent()
    bookmark = memcache.get(self._bookmarkKey(nID))

    if bookmark is None:
        bookmark = Bookmark.get_by_id(nID, owner)
        memcache.set(self._bookmarkKey(nID), bookmark)

    message = mail.EmailMessage(
        sender = owner.email,
        subject = "BookmarksBin shared link")

    message.to = email
    message.body = """
        Hello,

        A BookmarksBin user thought you may enjoy
        reading this:
        """

    message.body += bookmark.locator

    message.send()
    logging.info("Email to "+email+" sent")

def _shareBookmark(self):
    email = cgi.escape(self.request.get('recipient'))
    nID   = int(self.request.get('bookmarkID'))
    memcache.set(self._currentEmailTargetKey(), email)
    self._dispatchEmailTo(email, nID)
    self.renderPage('window_close.html', None)
```

The Mail API offers two ways of sending email to a third-party user: Python functions or the `EmailMessage` object wrapper. Both have identical functionality for sending plain text and multipart messages. The application may send messages from either its registered administrators or the current logged on user. Any errors will bounce to the sender's e-mail address.

Tip   The Mail API documentation, showing every method and attribute for the `EmailMessage` class and the `send_message()` function, is at `http://code.google.com/appengine/docs/mail/`.

Sending an e-mail is almost trivial: create an instance of the `EmailMessage` object or use the `send_mail()` function. It can be argued that `EmailMessage` objects are easier to maintain and visually scan, because they use discrete attributes for specifying the e-mail's attributes like `sender`, `to`, `cc`, `reply_to`, `subject`, and `body`, which are passed as a variable argument list when using `send_mail()`, like in Listing 8-2.

Listing 8-2. Using send_mail()

```
mail.send_mail(sender=owner.email,
    subject="BookmarksBin shared link",
    to=email,
    body=""" whatever """)
```

Neither `send_mail()` nor `EmailMessage.send()` return any values. E-mails are dispatched asynchronously; that's why errors are bounced to the sender.

The application logs an informational message by invoking `logging.info(aString)`. These messages are sent using the standard Python logging API, which becomes available to App Engine applications by adding the `import logging` statement to the code.

Using E-mail Templates

The example in the previous section inserts the e-mail body as a string. Building this string dynamically, either through formatters or by concatenation, is error-prone and results in verbose code that is harder to maintain.

The Django templates discussed in Chapter 4 can be used for rendering e-mail that just plugs values into the message body. Using these templates allows for more flexibility, since these files may be updated independently of the source code, and it results in improved application maintenance.

Listing 8-3. An E-mail Template

```
Hello,

{{ name }} thinks that you may enjoy reading this
document:

{{ locator }}

That link refers to:
{{ description }}.

Cheers!
```

The template can be as simple or as complex as the application requires, and the code depicted in Listing 8-4 resolves it.

Listing 8-4. Improved E-mail Dispatcher

```
# From bookmarksbin.py (partial)
import google.appengine.ext.webapp import template
   .
   .
   def _renderEmail(self, fileName, values):
     path = os.path.join(os.path.dirname(__file__),
        fileName)
```

```
    return template.render(path, values)

def _dispatchEmailTo(self, email, nID):
    .

    .

    values = dict(name = owner.nickname,
        locator = bookmark.locator,
        description = bookmark.description)

    .

    .

    message.body = self._renderEmail(
        "share_bookmark.eml", values)

    if message.is_initialized():
        message.send()
```

The template-rendering engine performs any value substitutions submitted to it. It returns a valid Python string that the application may process as required. Before sending the message, this method verifies that the e-mail message has been properly initialized by calling the is_initialized() instance method. This prevents App Engine from throwing an exception if the message's attributes haven't been properly initialized before handing it over to the MTA.

Sending Multipart E-mail Messages

Having e-mail templates is just a short step on the way to delivering multipart HTML, plain text, and attachments in messages. The Mail API supports all these features, as Listing 8-4 shows

Listing 8-4. Preparing and Sending a Multipart E-mail

```
def _dispatchEmailTo(self, email, nID):
    values = dict(name = owner.nickname,
        locator = bookmark.locator,
        description = bookmark.description)

    attachments = [
```

```
        ("instructions.txt", instructionsBlob),
        ("movie.jpg", moviePoster)]

    message = mail.EmailMessage(
        sender = owner.email,
        subject = "BookmarksBin shared link")

    message.to = email
    message.body = self._renderEmail(
        "share_bookmark.eml", values)
    message.body = self._renderEmail(
        "share_bookmark.html", values)

    message.attachments = attachments

    message.send()
    logging.info("Email to "+email+" sent")
```

An HTML version of the message is provided by simply specifying a rendered string from a template, much like displaying a response in an event handler. Inline images could be defined with the `cid:` (content ID) tag and delivered along with the message as attachments.

Caution   Many spam filters mark HTML-only e-mails as positives and send them to the bit bucket. If the application must send HTML messages, ensure that a plain text message with the same text is also provided to avoid triggering false positives and to ensure that users get the intended message.

Attachments are specified as a list of two-value tuples. Each tuple contains the file name in its first element and the payload as a byte string in the second.

App Engine applications don't have direct access to the file system in which they run, so storing them in `db.BlobProperty` properties is considered a good practice. Although BLOBs aren't searchable by themselves, they may be combined with other properties in queries, and the entities that contain them can be cached for maximum efficiency.

Only the file types listed in Table 8-1 are allowed in attachments for security purposes. The case-sensitive file's extension must match one of the allowed types. The Mail API determines the appropriate MIME type based on the file extension as well.

Table 8-1. Allowed Attachment Types

MIME TYPE	EXTENSION
image/x-ms-bmp	.bmp
text/css	.css
text/comma-separated-values	.csv
image/gif	.gif
text/html	.html, .htm
image/jpeg	.jpeg, .jpg, .jpe
application/pdf	.pdf
image/png	.png
application/rss+xml	.rss
text/plain	.txt, .text, .asc, .diff, .pot
image/tiff	.tif, .tiff
image/vnd.wap.wbmp	.wbmp

Validating E-mail Addresses

The `is_email_valid()` function validates an e-mail address and returns a Boolean value. Its companion function, `check_email_valid()`, performs the same test but throws an `InvalidEmailError` if it fails.

Given the runtime quotas imposed by App Engine, it's almost always advisable to perform this check via JavaScript in the browser rather than call these functions. They should be called only when validating e-mail addresses obtained through programmatic, nonbrowser means (e.g., from a CSV list). If the application uses either of these functions, it can also elucidate the cause by invoking the `invalid_email_reason()` and passing it the offending e-mail address; it will return a string description of why the address fails to pass.

Using the Fetch URL API

Web applications flourish when they communicate with other applications or services that can enhance their feature sets. App Engine offers a simple URL fetching API that may be used for making RESTful service calls, retrieving assets from remote sites, or accessing third-party RSS data feeds.

The complete API consists of a single function, `fetch()`, which returns a response object with all the pertinent data regarding the call. `fetch()` implements HTTP 1.1 request methods GET, POST, PUT, and DELETE as constants in the App Engine `urlfetch` module. It allows a caller to provide these parameters:

- The URL to invoke.

- A payload for the POST or PUT methods.

- A subset of possible HTTP headers. Not all HTTP headers are allowed to prevent malicious uses.

- A Boolean setting that follows 3xx redirects. The function will follow up to five consecutive redirection levels and return the data as if it were at the requested location. If not set, the function will return the redirect payload from the first URL, including headers, back to the invoker.

- An attribute for specifying whether content may be truncated if data exceeds the maximum response size.

Tip   Check out the complete URL Fetch API at `http://code` `.google.com/appengine/docs/urlfetch/`.

Unlike the Mail API services, `fetch()` is always synchronous. Any URL or URI invoked by the application must be spry, or the application's request handler itself may time out.

The response object is an instance of the private class `_URLFetchResult`, defined in the URL Fetch API module. The documentation calls it a generic response object and lists these as its public attributes:

- `content`: A string corresponding to the server's response

- `content_was_truncated`: A Boolean set to `True` if the request allows truncated responses and the payload exceeded the maximum size

- `headers`: A mapping of names/values corresponding to the HTTP response headers

- `status_code`: The HTTP request status code (e.g., 200, 302, 404, or 503)

`fetch()` calls throw exceptions in case of failure in addition to the HTTP status code reported in the call. The API describes the conditions that throw exceptions such as `InvalidURLError` or `DownloadError`.

SUPPORTED PORTS, PROTOCOLS, AND CERTIFICATES

The URL Fetch API supports access to only ports 80 (HTTP) and 443 (HTTPS) and their associated protocols. Keep in mind that, although HTTPS requests are supported, the `fetch()` API cannot authenticate the host and it accepts any certificate, whether that certificate comes from a legitimate signing authority (e.g., Verisign) or is self-signed. It will fetch the resource without validating its domain of origin.

Calling a Web Service

Fetch URL is an ideal mechanism for calling web services. Services may be implemented through common protocols, such as servlet calls, REST, or SOAP. Some of these protocols have significant overhead, like SOAP, because they require additional libraries or processor-heavy XML parsing routines. Others may not be suitable for inclusion in App Engine applications because their libraries want to manage the URI connection themselves. In general, `fetch()` works best with RESTful or servlet API calls, because they have low overhead and the service consumer can decide how much of the payload to process during the call. Complex calls with high payload processing times may result in hitting the App Engine resource quotas faster.

Users may not be able to share a bookmark from the BookmarksBin application if the URL is long, because some e-mail clients (most notoriously Microsoft's Entourage and Outlook) render the URLs unclickable by splitting the lines at a fixed number of columns. Some spam-filtering software sees long URLs as threats and may eliminate a message in its entirety.

URI OR URL?

Universal Resource Identifiers (URIs) are the means for accessing Internet resources. A Universal Resource Locator (URL) is a form of URI that expresses an address that maps onto an access algorithm using specific network protocols. "URI" is the term preferred in technical documentation, but "URL" is most common in popular usage. This discussion will use "URL" when talking about an identifier pointing at a web page intended for view with a web browser. "URI" will be used for services and all cases where the resource may be something other than a web page or its components.

`http://www.is.gd` is a service that transforms a URI into a shorter version of itself and redirects requests to the resource when queried.

Suppose that `http://bookmarksbin.appspot.com` is too long to fit into the screen of a mobile device. Provide this URI to `is.gd` and get instead a much shorter version: `http://is.gd/6uwN` that can fit in a tiny screen or that is unlikely to be truncated by a buggy e-mail client.

`is.gd` offers a web page for interactive use and a simple API for programmatic access. BookmarksBin uses the latter to compress bookmarks before sharing by leveraging the `is.gd` service call in Listing 8-5.

Listing 8-5. Calling a Web Service with fetch()

```
# From bookmarksbin.py (partial)
from urllib import urlencode
from google.appengine.api.urlfetch import fetch
.
.
  def _compressURL(self, aLocator):
    ISGD_URI = 'http://is.gd/api.php?longurl='
    l = urlencode({'l': aLocator})

    try:
      result = fetch(ISGD_URI+l[2:])
      if 200 == result.status_code:
        return result.content
      else:
        return aLocator
    except:
      return aLocator

  def _dispatchEmailTo(self, email, nID):
    .
    .
    values = dict(name = owner.nickname,
        locator = self._compressURL(bookmark.locator),
        description = bookmark.description)
```

```
message = mail.EmailMessage(
    sender = owner.email,
    subject = "BookmarksBin shared link")

message.to = email
message.body = self._renderEmail(
    "share_bookmark.eml", values)

message.send()
```

_compressURL() creates a valid is.gd service call by appending the bookmark locator to the service URI. Note that it's necessary to URL encode the locator before submitting it to the service.

Most of the examples in this book ignored exception handling because of typographical space constraints. fetch() calls, however, rely on third-party services with variable service levels and may time out or otherwise fail in catastrophic ways. Always catch any errors dispatched by calls to fetch() and provide graceful degradation.

Fetching a Resource from Another Site

BookmarksBin entries could assist the user in quick identification by providing a visual cue of what a bookmark may contain without forcing that user to read the description. fetch() can be used for retrieving a hosting site's favicon.ico file and displaying it next to the bookmark description, as in Listing 8-6.

Listing 8-6. Fetching a Site Icon

```
# From bookmarksbin.py (partial)

from urlparse import urlsplit
    .

    .

def _fetchIconFor(self, aLocator):
    components = urlsplit(aLocator)
```

```
      iconRef      = components[0]
      iconRef     += "://"+components[1]
      iconRef     += "/favicon.ico"
      icon = None

      try:
         logging.info("Fetching "+iconRef)
         result = fetch(iconRef)
         if 200 == result.status_code:
            icon = result.content
      except:
         logging.info("Failed to fetch "+iconRef)

      return icon

   def _addBookmark(self):
      tagNames = self.request.get_all('tags')
      locator  = cgi.escape(self.request.get('locator'))

      bookmark = Bookmark(
         parent = Owner.getCurrent(),
         description = cgi.escape(
            self.request.get('description')),
         favIcon = self._fetchIconFor(locator),
         locator = locator,
         title = None,
         owner = Owner.getCurrent())
         .
         .
```

A `Bookmark` entity stores the icon in the `favIcon db.BlobProperty` for later manipulation or display. To obtain the icon, the `_fetchIconFor()` method builds a URL dynamically based on the one for the bookmark and attempts to fetch it. The call may fail because favorite icons aren't mandatory, or because of network latency, or any other reasons associated with HTTP transfers from a third party.

Manipulating Images

Google App Engine offers the ability to manipulate images using the same infrastructure as Picasa Web Albums for some common image manipulation operations:

- Resizing

- Flipping

- Rotating

- Cropping

- Automatic "I'm feeling lucky" optimizer for brightness, contrast, and color

The API supports operations on BMP, GIF, ICO, JPEG, PNG, and TIFF images—the common formats for web application development.

Required for Development: The Python Imaging Library (PIL)

The development server implements local functionality of the Images API through the use of the Python Imaging Library (PIL). PIL adds to the Python runtime image-processing capabilities geared toward archival and batch processing applications. App Engine supports the subset of PIL necessary for implementing its main functionality. Image manipulation is processor intensive, so preserve resources to keep low application usage quotas and apply these APIs judiciously.

PIL isn't part of the standard Python distribution or the Google App Engine SDK and must be installed as a separate component. Check out these web pages for more information:

- `http://code.google.com/appengine/docs/images/` `installingPIL.html`: Google App Engine installation instructions for OS X, Linux, and Windows

- `http://www.pythonware.com/products/pil/index.htm`: PythonWare's PIL official site

The development application server shows this warning message if PIL isn't installed during start up:

```
WARNING 05:05:41,746 dev_appserver.py] Could not
   initialize images API; you are likely missing the
   Python "PIL" module. ImportError: No module
   named PIL
```

Please ensure that PIL is installed and that the warning is gone before trying the image manipulation examples in the rest of this chapter.

PIL Installation Pitfalls

PIL installation in any of the supported operating systems isn't straightforward. This third-party module requires more third-party libraries, and it doesn't require the same things or in the same order across multiple operating systems. PIL was installed in all three supported operating systems (OS X, Linux, and Windows) and although the specific steps vary significantly for each, the process is the same for all. Here's a list of some common issues that you should try to avoid:

- Installation using package managers is nice, but in my experience, four out of five different installations of either PIL itself or its support libraries failed. apt-get was the only package manager that worked without glitches. If possible, install from source files.

- Get the PIL `Images-version.tar.gz` or `Images-version.zip` file, and install it to a working directory.

- Read the README file, and ensure that every prerequisite is met; all environments require having some library or other already installed in the system before installing PIL itself, and the required libraries aren't the same across operating systems. OS X, for example, requires libjpeg and FREETYPE. Windows, on the other hand, requires modifying the installation script itself for the admin user.

- Get the required libraries, and install them from source as well, following their respective instructions.

- Perform any recommended tweaks specific to the target installation environment.

- Install PIL by following the instructions in the INSTALL or README file enclosed with the source download. The command sequence is similar to

```
python setup.py build_ext -i; python selftest.py ; if [[
  "$?" = "0" ]]; then sudo python setup.py install; fi.
```

- Run the dev_appserver.py program; the warning from the previous section will be gone, and the application can now call the Image API.

Using the Images API

Every Bookmark entity stores a copy of the favicon.ico file from the original site to help as a visual cue for easier identification of its associated site. Figure 8-2 shows each bookmark's site icon next to its entry in the list.

Figure 8-2. Favorite icons displayed along with a bookmark

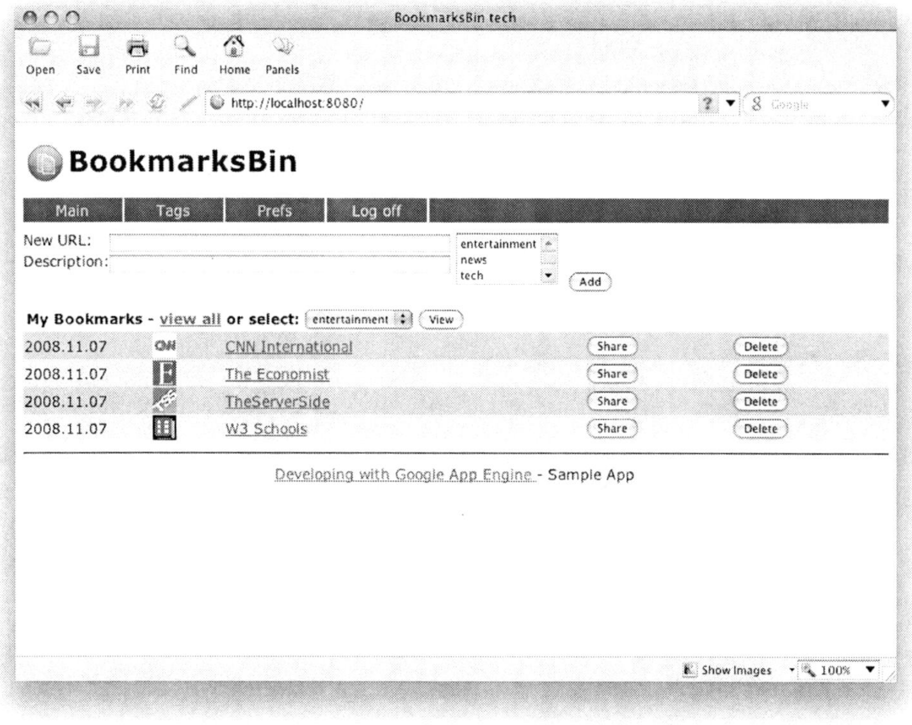

Favorite icon files are 16×16–pixel images. Their default size appears too small when displayed along the bookmark information. Listing 8-7 shows how to use the Images API calls to resize the image before storing it with the rest of the bookmark's data.

Listing 8-7. Modifying an Image

```
# From bookmarksbin.py (partial)
from google.appengine.api import images
    .
    .
  def _fetchIconFor(self, aLocator):
      .
    try:
```

```
            logging.info("Fetching "+iconRef)
            result = fetch(iconRef)
            if 200 == result.status_code:
                icon = result.content
                icon = images.resize(icon, 24, 24)
                icon = images.im_feeling_lucky(icon,
                    output_encoding = images.ICO)
        except:
            logging.info("Failed to fetch "+iconRef)

        return icon
```

The icon is resized and optimized for contrast and color using the
im_feeling_lucky() call. The application can call the functions in the
images API, like in Listing 8-7, or use the Image object wrapper instead, as
in Listing 8-8.

Listing 8-8. Using the Image Class

```
icon = Image(result.content)
icon.resize(24, 24)
icon = Image(icon.execute_transform(images.ICO))
return icon.im_feeling_lucky()
```

The Image API is rather awkward. First, most transformations won't take
effect until calling execute_transform(). Then, the
im_feeling_lucky() method transforms the image independently of calls
to execute_transform(). Last, transforms are applied in the requested
order and only once per image, per execute_transform() call. Using the
Image API functions may be a better option than the Image wrapper,
because the wrapper uses imperative calls and each transform is applied as
it's called without having to worry about execution order.

The complete icon persists to the Datastore a BLOB. Listing 8-9 shows
how to use the image from the output template. It requires a handler that
fetches the appropriate icon from Memcache or from the Datastore, since
the icons can't be saved to App Engine's file system.

Listing 8-9. Using the Icon in HTML Output

```
<td>
  <img src=
    {% if bookmark.favIcon %}
      "icon?id={{ bookmark.id_or_name }}"
    {% else %}
      "./qm.png" width="24" height"24"
    {% endif %}
  border="0" />
</td>
```

The icon handler is implemented in the IconServer from Listing 8-10. It takes a bookmark ID as an argument, fetches the corresponding Bookmark entity, and returns the BLOB as an image.

Listing 8-10. IconServer Implementation

```
# From bookmarksbin.py
class IconServer(AppHandler):
  def get(self):
    nID = int(self.request.get('id'))
    if nID == None:
      nID = -1
    bookmark = memcache.get(
        bookmarkKey(nID))

    if bookmark is None:
      bookmark = Bookmark.get_by_id(nID,
          Owner.getCurrent())
      memcache.set(bookmarkKey(nID), bookmark)

    if bookmark.favIcon:
      self.response.headers['Content-Type'] = \
          'image/ico'
      self.response.out.write(bookmark.favIcon)
    else:
      logging.info("Invalid icon req "+str(nID))
      self.response.out.write("No icon")
```

This event handler shows how to return content that's different from the default HTML. The application may set response headers by adding them to the response's HTTP header dictionary. The icon's file representation in the BLOB is passed verbatim to the browser for display.

The Images API can be used in any application that requires image alterations on the server side. Keep in mind that these manipulations are costly in terms of processor cycles, so it's better to keep them to a minimum.

Summary

Google App Engine platform offers basic tools for sending e-mail, fetching files from other servers, and manipulating images. The number of basic APIs and services like these may increase as App Engine matures. These basic APIs can be combined to call Google Data Services, Amazon services, or any other web-enabled service or resource that App Engine can access. Because the application code relies on external services for implementing desired functionality, keep in mind that the world is an asynchronous, error-prone place. Calls to external services must be profiled for performance and provide graceful degradation if the third-party service is unavailable or fails.

This concludes the programming portion of this book. The last chapter will present the App Engine Admin Console, where the application administrators get to view their application's performance and modify some of its hosting parameters and characteristics.

Chapter 9: Managing the Application

The Admin Console is the web interface used for managing App Engine applications, and it provides functions for

- Creating and registering new applications, as described in Chapter 2

- Managing domains and subdomains

- Analyzing traffic and data logs

- Managing the Datastore and indexes

- Managing version control and deployment

- Inviting other developers or application administrators to participate in a project

Managing Applications

Application management for Google App Engine is rather limited during the preview release. Google may increase the number of features after the service is released for general availability, perhaps with a subscription or usage payment model. Until then, however, applications have several limitations. The bounds aren't arbitrary; they are derived from the free nature of the service and the limited resources allocated to it during this preview release.

Accessing the Application Management Console

The application management console is tied to the each App Engine registered developer's account. Developers can access the console through either of these URLs:

- `http://appengine.google.com`

- `http://www.appspot.com`

There is no distinction between a developer and an application administrator. One or more developers can work on a project; the only requirements are that each developer has a valid Google Account ID and is registered with App Engine.

Caution If you are a developer outside of the US, Canada, or Japan, beware that the registration process includes sending a validation code to a mobile number via SMS. Although SMS is available in almost every country on Earth, Google's services may not be able to send messages to a few carriers in some countries.

Last, each registration is limited to one account per mobile number, not to the developer's Gmail account only. Trying to register two developers under the same phone number also gives an error.

Restrictions on Creating an Application

The process for creating an application was covered in detail in the "Publishing to the Web" section from Chapter 2.

App Engine allows only ten active applications per user at any given time, and there is no way to remove an application after it has been created. The counter is global and tied to the developer's account, so there is no way to fudge the count other than going through the pain of creating a new Gmail account and finding another mobile number to receive the authentication message.

Several users in the App Engine discussion boards have posted what they believe is a hack for bypassing this restriction: create a secondary account, add the developer to the project, and then remove the project from its original creation account. This trick doesn't work, as shown in Figure 9-1.

Figure 9-1. My Applications Listed in the application console

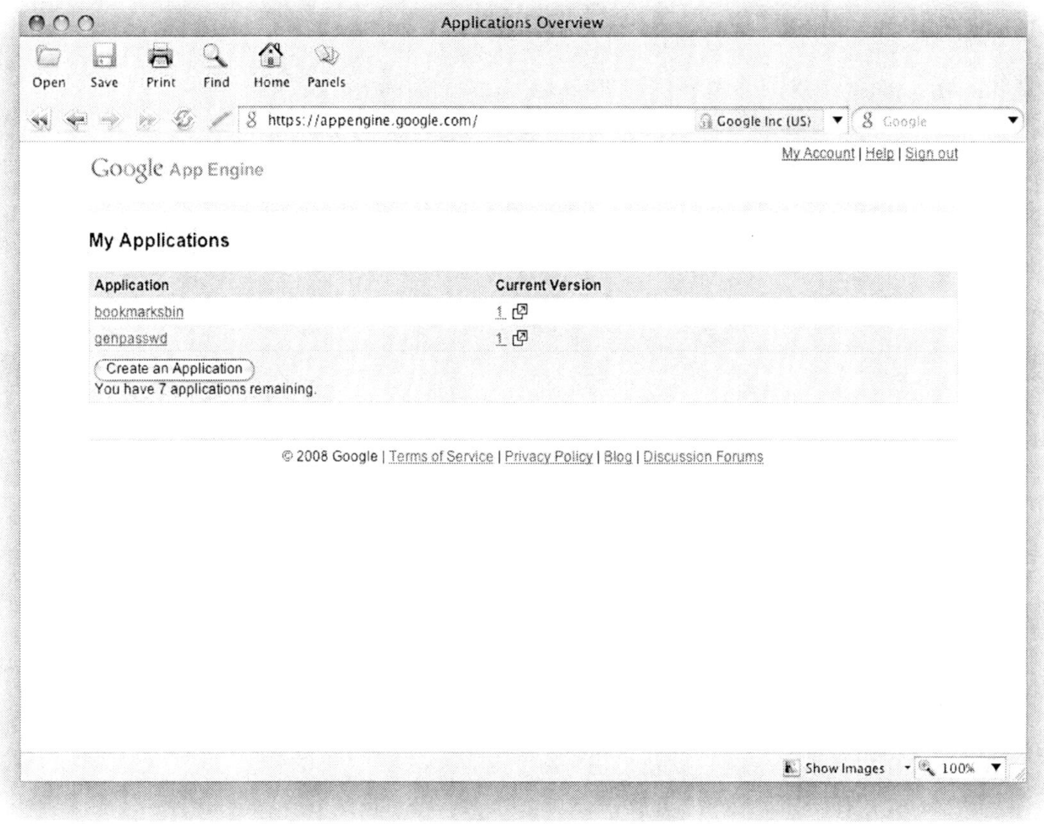

The list shows only the two active applications used for the examples in this book. The App Engine console indicates, however, that this user has seven applications remaining. The other sample application was shared with a secondary user, and the original was removed from the list. Though the original user can no longer access the application, it still counts toward the ten-applications-per-developer quota.

Other restrictions regarding applications follow:

- The application name must be registered only at creation time and cannot be changed.

- Authentication options must be set during creation.

Changing the Application Configuration

Each application appears in its own dashboard screen and has one or more developers or administrators associated with it. These developers or administrators may modify a few parameters for the application, namely these:

- *Domain in which the application runs*: For example, BookmarksBin is accessible both from its stand-alone domain via `http://www .bookmarksbin.com` and from the App Engine domain at `http:// bookmarksbin.appspot.com`.

- *Application name displayed during sign-in*: The rest of the page isn't customizable at this time, but users will know that the Google Accounts login page in front of them is associated with the application they're trying to access.

- *List of developers who can modify and manage the application*: Everyone on the list must have a valid Google App Engine development account.

- *Application version*: Select the currently active application version from among those that have been uploaded already.

Using the Application Administration Logs

Each activity listed in this section creates an audit trail that may be inspected via the application's administration logs. These logs show every activity carried out from the moment that the application was registered until its current state in App Engine, as shown in Figure 9-2.

Figure 9-2. Administration logs for BookmarksBin

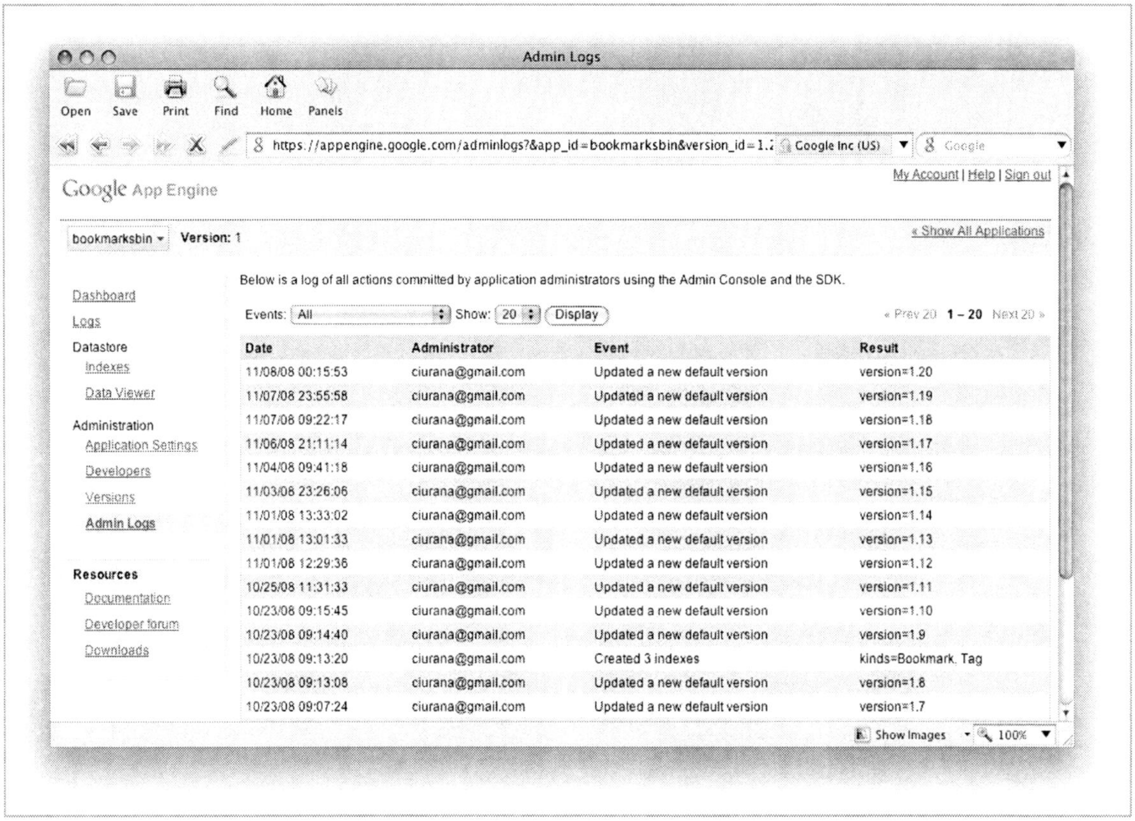

An administrator may filter these logs according to several criteria to, for example, view only uploads, indexes updates, or application name changes.

The Dashboard

The Dashboard provides a bird's eye view of all the application's runtime activity over a fixed period of time. The default period is the last 24 hours for the preview edition, though it'll likely be configurable in future releases of App Engine.

Figure 9-3 shows the Dashboard's default view, displaying the number of requests per second, CPU and data transfer usage and storage, e-mails sent, and so on.

Figure 9-3. The Dashboard

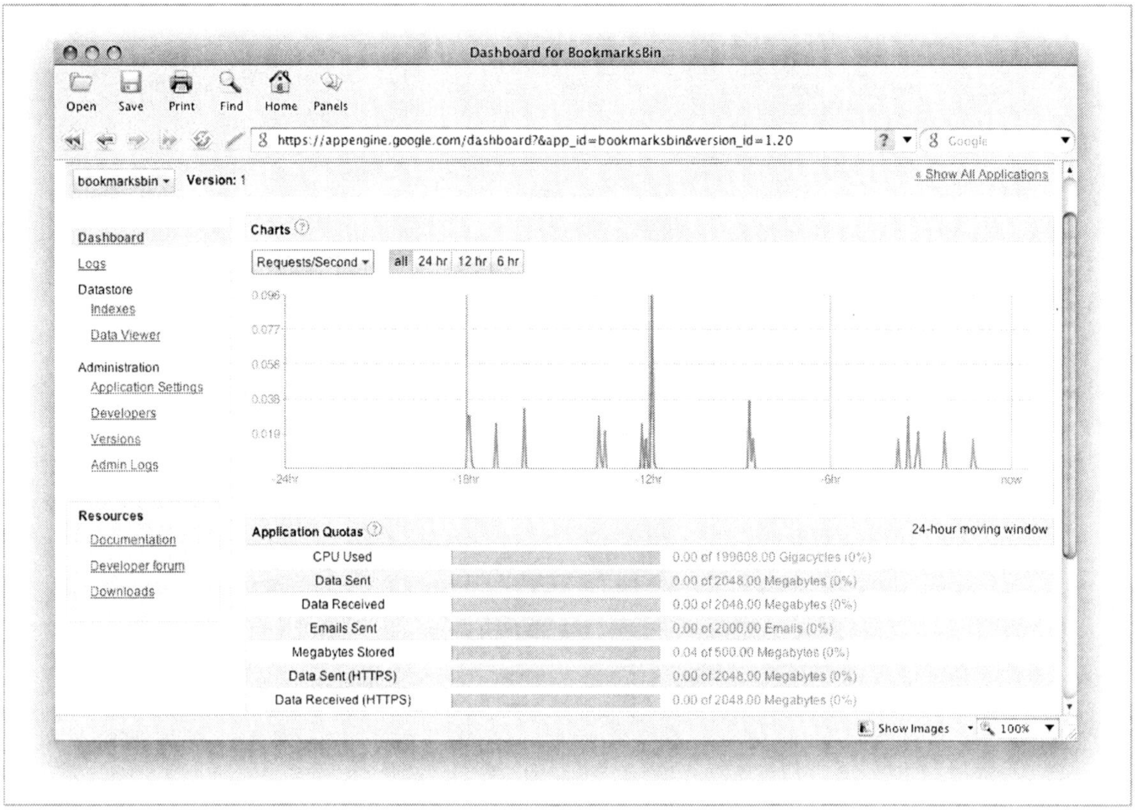

The Dashboard also displays count and percentage information about errors per URI, current load, and reports on the usage and application quotas for CPU, data usage, and storage.

The Runtime Logs

The administration console offers the ability to display the application's runtime logs for analysis. The logs are not in standard Apache format, and they are impossible to download for offline analysis from this view.

Each log line is summarized with a time stamp, the action performed against the application, and a toggle for showing/hiding all the details of each operation, as shown in Figure 9-4.

Figure 9-4. Application runtime logs

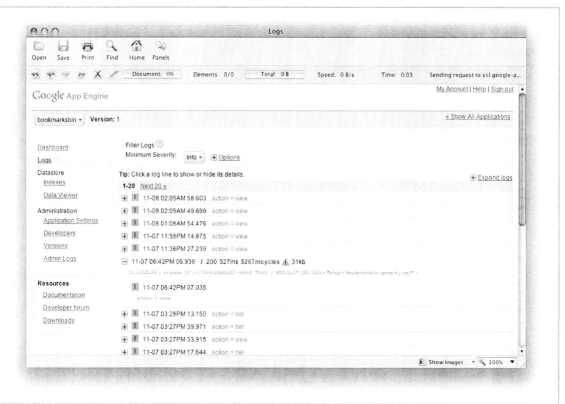

Log entries may be expanded individually or in bulk, and the administrator may filter them to list entries with specific logging levels such as info, debug, and warn.

Offline Log Analysis

Developers may request the application's logs using the appcfg.py tool. In the example in Listing 9-1, the user is requesting the last two days of logging activity, with a severity level of DEBUG or greater, and filtering any empty lines that may appear in the log.

Listing 9-1. Local Extraction and Analysis of a Runtime Log

```
12345678901234567890123456789012345678901234567890123456
7890
appcfg.py --num_days=2 --severity=0 request_logs \
bookmarksbin bookmarksbin.log; cat bookmarksbin.log \
 | awk '!/^$/' | more
Loaded authentication cookies from
/Users/ciurana/.appcfg_cookies
Downloading request logs for bookmarksbin 1.1.
Copying request logs to 'bookmarksbin.log'.
Copied 20 records.
74.0.125.28 - ciurana [07/11/2008:09:33:26 -0800]
"POST / HTTP/1.1" 200 31684
"http://bookmarksbin.appspot.com/" -
        1:1226079206.493546 action = view
74.0.125.28 - ciurana [07/11/2008:10:21:13 -0800]
"POST / HTTP/1.1" 200 31518
"http://bookmarksbin.appspot.com/" -
        1:1226082073.049069 action = view
63.114.26.15 - ciurana [07/11/2008:11:17:29 -0800]
"POST / HTTP/1.1" 200 31518
"http://bookmarksbin.appspot.com/" -
        1:1226085449.741612 action = view
74.0.125.28 - ciurana [07/11/2008:13:44:17 -0800]
"POST / HTTP/1.1" 200 116983
"http://bookmarksbin.appspot.com/" -
        1:1226094256.439547 action = add
```

Logs and Application Quotas

The logging data for the App Engine preview appears to conflict with the quota reports in the Dashboard. This conflict may be the result of having too few servers in the backend or the ongoing evolution of the App Engine platform.

In general, it's probably a good idea to believe the data in the activity logs over the Dashboard quota reports, since activity logs show the completion time and the resource consumption per operation and will be more helpful for tuning.

Viewing Active Indexes

Figure 9-5 depicts the BookmarksBin active indexes and their statuses. As you recall from Chapter 6, compounded indexes are defined in the `app.yaml` file and uploaded or updated using the `appcfg.py` tool.

Figure 9-5. Indexes view

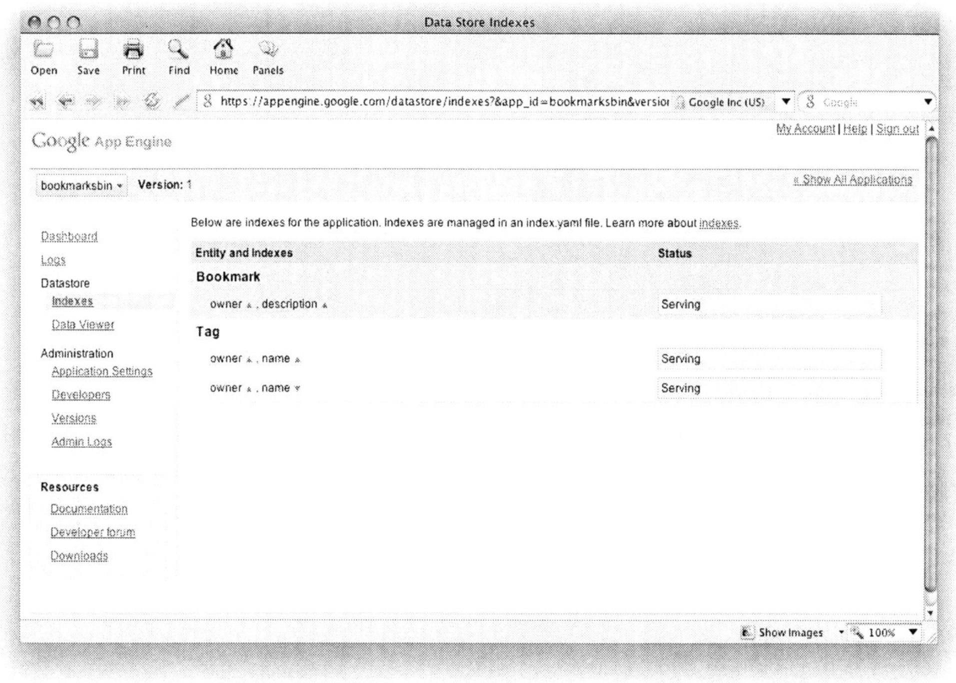

An index status may be Building right after an index update or Serving if everything is working fine, or it may reflect an error in processing. Errors aren't cleared using the administration console. Unused indexes aren't automatically deleted. Instead, the developer or administrator must run `appcfg.py -vacuum_index` command to help clean them up.

Any indexes defined in App Engine that aren't also present in `index.yaml` may be safely deleted.

Viewing and Manipulating Datastore Objects

The Data Viewer in Figure 9-6 shows all the Datastore entities in use by BookmarksBin.

Figure 9-6. The Data Viewer

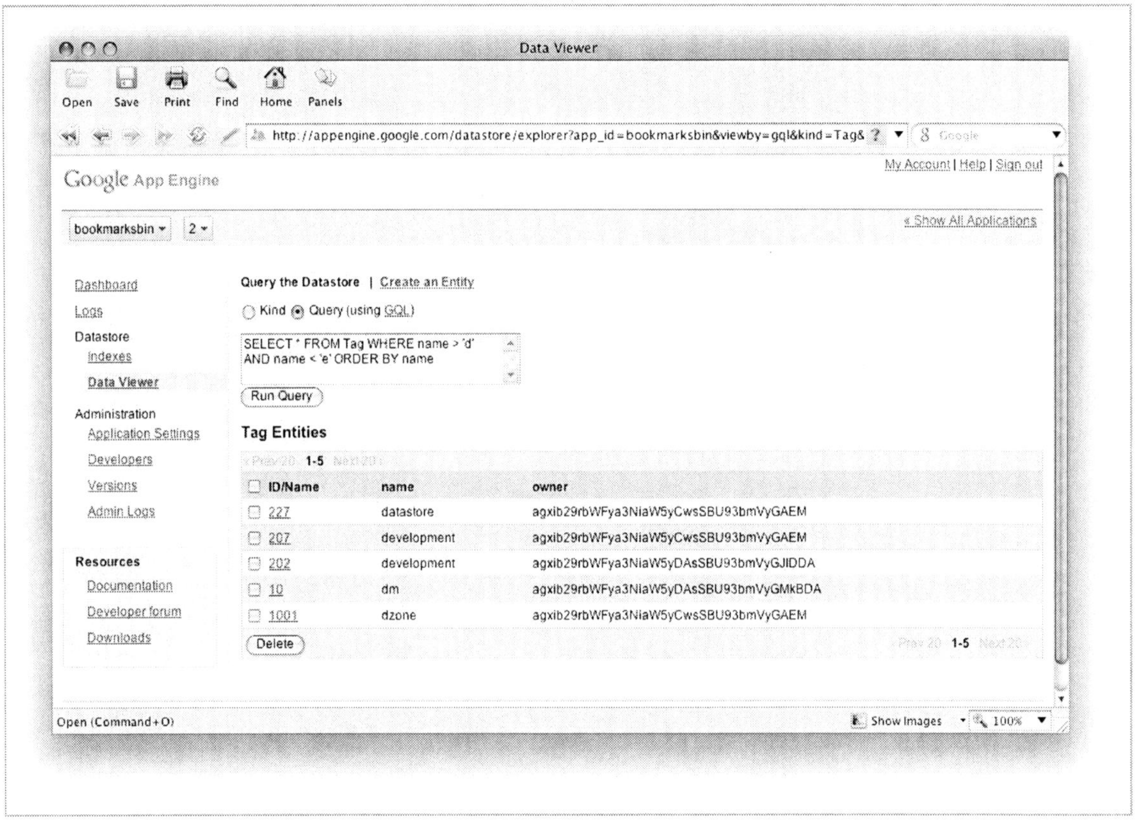

The Data Viewer acts as an interactive window for manipulating Datastore entities or their properties through a web interface. Users may create, review, or alter any entity of a given kind. Though it's not the most effective way to manage entities, it's a very useful tool for troubleshooting the application without having to resort to custom coding to address an issue. It's even possible to run simple GQL queries directly from the Data Viewer.

Using the Development Console

Since development takes place for the most part on the developer's system, rather than in the App Engine hosts, the SDK provides a Development Console (see Figure 9-7) with functionality similar to the Data Viewer.

Figure 9-7. Inspecting Memcache in the development console

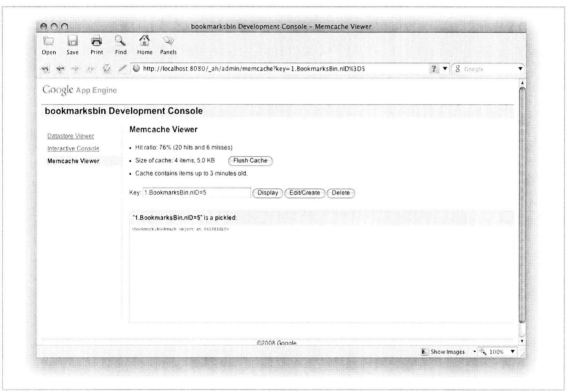

The Development Console runs from the `dev_appserver.py` local development server, and it's accessed through the `http://localhost:8080/_ah/admin` URL. It provides the ability to inspect and manipulate Datastore entities and Memcache objects and to execute ad hoc Python code that runs in the same address space as the application itself.

Summary

The Admin Console and its cousin the Development Console provide essential functionality for creating and deploying applications, managing the users who can update and manage the code, profile applications, analyze logs, monitor the Datastore, and administer resources. Although these consoles continue to evolve, they ease application administration by enabling both Web-based, interactive operations and offline analysis and configuration in tandem with the SDK.

The journey of *Developing with Google App Engine* concludes here. From writing the first greeting program to coding a full-blown application, from working with standard Python to implementing complex data manipulations involving Memcache and the Datastore, and from entering a few simple commands in a terminal to managing thousands of entities and runtime monitoring feeds in the application console, you now have the tools to create elegant and scalable applications with a low cost of entry and with short inception-to-deployment times. Good luck in your next journey and happy coding!

Related Titles

Here are a few additional titles that you might find helpful; all are available as eBooks:

Beginning Google Maps Applications with PHP and Ajax: From Novice to Professional by Michael Purvis, Jeffrey Sambells, and Cameron Turner (Apress, 2006): This is the first book to comprehensively introduce Google's popular mapping API. This book shows you how to create practical, location-based applications that encourage users to interact with the service, add their own information, and dynamically mark up maps.

Accelerated GWT: Building Enterprise Google Web Toolkit Applications by Vipul Gupta (Apress, 2008): Serious Java developers wanting to write Ajax applications using GWT can expect a fast-paced, yet thorough, introduction to GWT from Java expert Vipul Gupta. Without superfluous introductions to Ajax or JavaScript, you'll learn to incorporate Ajax capabilities into your web applications quickly, without sacrificing sound development principles.

Beginning Google Web Toolkit: From Novice to Professional by Bram Smeets, Uri Boness, and Roald Bankras (Apress, 2008): Learn to build rich, user-friendly web applications using a popular Java-based Ajax web framework, the Google Web Toolkit. The authors will guide you through the complete development of a GWT front-end application with a no-nonsense, down-to-earth approach.

Google Maps Mashups with Google Mapplets by Michael Young (Apress, 2008): This is the book that geo-mashups developers will need to create Web 2.0 applications based on Google's new mapplets technology. It presents both a complete guide to the new standard and the practical how-to that developers seek. Written by Michael Young, an award-winning, new technology expert from *The New York Times*, the book is both authoritative and eminently usable.

Beginning Google Maps Mashups with Mapplets, KML, and GeoRSS by Sterling Udell (Apress, 2008): This is a beginner's guide to creating web mashups using Google mapping technology. This book is a single-source primer to displaying data on Google Maps and covers both mapplets and the Google Maps API. It is everything you need to start participating in the Geographic Web.

Google Guice: Agile Lightweight Dependency Injection Framework by Robbie Vanbrabant (Apress, 2008): This book will not only tell you "how," it will also tell you "why" and "why not," so that all the knowledge you gain will be as widely applicable as possible. Filled with examples and background information, this book is an invaluable addition to your knowledge of modern agile Java.

Copyright

Developing with Google App Engine

ISBN-13 (paperback): 978-1-4302-1831-9

ISBN-13 (electronic): 978-1-4302-1832-6

Trademarked names may appear in this book. Rather than use a trademark symbol with every occurrence of a trademarked name, we use the names only in an editorial fashion and to the benefit of the trademark owner, with no intention of infringement of the trademark.

Distributed to the book trade in the United States by Springer-Verlag New York, Inc., 233 Spring Street, 6th Floor, New York, NY 10013, and outside the United States by Springer-Verlag GmbH & Co. KG, Tiergartenstr. 17, 69112 Heidelberg, Germany.

In the United States: phone 1-800-SPRINGER, fax 201-348-4505, e-mail orders@springer-ny.com, or visit http://www.springer-ny.com. Outside the United States: fax +49 6221 345229, e-mail orders@springer.de, or visit http://www.springer.de.

For information on translations, please contact Apress directly at 2855 Telegraph Ave, Suite 600, Berkeley, CA 94705. Phone 510-549-5930, fax 510-549-5939, e-mail info@apress.com, or visit http://www.apress.com.